D1330279

Caring For God's People

CARING FOR GOD'S PEOPLE

A Handbook for Elders and Ministers on Pastoral Care

Stewart Matthew · Ken Lawson

THE SAINT ANDREW PRESS · EDINBURGH

First published in 1989 by
THE SAINT ANDREW PRESS
121 George Street, Edinburgh
Copyright © 1989 Stewart Matthew and Kenneth Lawson
ISBN 0 7152 0634 6

All rights reserved. No part of this publication may be
reproduced or transmitted in any form or by any means
electronic or mechanical, including photocopy, recording, or
any information storage and retrieval system, without
permission in writing from the publisher. This book is sold
subject to the condition that it shall not, by way of trade or
otherwise, be lent, re-sold, hired out or otherwise circulated
without the publisher's prior consent.

British Library Cataloguing in Publication Data
Matthew, Stewart
  Caring for God's people : a handbook for elders and
  ministers on pastoral care.
  1. Christian Church. Pastoral work
  I. Title II. Lawson, Ken
  253

  ISBN 0-7152-0634-6

This book was set in 11/12pt Plantin

Typeset by Print Origination (NW) Ltd, Liverpool
Printed by Bell & Bain Ltd, Glasgow

Contents

About the writers   6

Introduction   7

Some terminology   8

Dedication   9

1   How do I come to be doing this?   11

2   Getting started   25

3   Learning to care   38

4   Praying with those whom we visit   55

5   Situations we face as elders   62

6   Taking care of yourself   78

7   Caring for each other as elders   87

8   Developing a pastoral strategy   104

9   A caring congregation   110

On the road   123

Acknowledgements   127

About the writers

Ken Lawson is a member of the staff of the Church of Scotland's Department of Education. He has particular responsibility for the important work of its Group Relations Sub-Committee. He specialises in providing training and trainers in various areas of human relationships and spiritual development.

He was minister of St Mungo's, Cumbernauld, from 1972 to 1984 and before that minister of the South Church, Paisley.

Stewart Matthew is also a member of the staff of the Church of Scotland's Department of Education. He has done much to focus attention on the importance of the eldership, producing resource materials and providing training opportunities for elders. He is the co-author of another handbook for elders on session management, entitled *Leading God's People* (The Saint Andrew Press).

He was minister of St Ninian's, Bellfield, in Kilmarnock from 1969 to 1979 and before that was a teacher of Religious Education at Swinton Comprehensive School in Yorkshire.

Both of them work from St Colm's Education Centre and College, Edinburgh.

Introduction

The role of elders is to lead and develop the lifestyle of their congregation. Within this there is often given to elders the important work of caring for a number of members of their congregation. Sadly many elders receive little support in their work of caring and little or no help to develop their caring skills. It is also sad, and perhaps not unconnected, that many Church members today have a low expectation level regarding the pastoral role of their elder. Many elders share this low expectation regarding their caring role.

In *Caring for God's People* we look at the elder's pastoral role in the context of life and faith, the Church and the shared ministry of all who belong to God's Church. Emphasis is put on relationship-building, with listening as the basic skill required of the district elder and modelling God's care the objective.

Practical help is given regarding building relationships, tackling difficult situations which elders have to face, the part prayer plays in the elder's ministry and how to take care of oneself.

The concluding chapters deal with:

- The development of a caring Session (one in which the elders have a real concern for each other) which affects greatly the quality of care they are able to offer, individually and collectively, to other people.

- The development of a more effective pastoral strategy than the typical one-person/one-district strategy. The development of a caring congregation in which the members care for each other and together care for the world beyond their congregation—caring for *all* God's people

Some terminology

Church of Scotland		Presbyterian Church in Ireland		Presbyterian Church of Wales		United Reformed Church
Kirk Session or Session	=	Kirk Session	=	Elders' Meeting	=	Elders' Meeting
Elder's District	=	Elder's District	=	Elder's District	=	Elder's Group
Presbytery	=	Presbytery	=	Presbytery	=	District Council
Synod	=	Synod	=	The Association	=	Province
General Assembly	=	General Assembly	=	General Assembly	=	General Assembly

Using this book

We hope this book will be of use to the elders and ministers of the different Presbyterian denominations and to other people who are involved in caring for people.

Throughout the book there are suggestions 'For further reading' to help the reader follow up a topic of interest. Listed under the heading 'For thinking through' there are questions for the reader to think through. Most of them can be shared with fellow-elders.

Dedication

To the elders of God's people

1 How do I come to be doing this?

As an elder you have knocked on the door of a home of a member of your congregation. As you stand on that doorstep, waiting for the door to open, perhaps you ask yourself '*How* do I come to be doing this?'

No doubt many an elder asks himself or herself that question, and other questions like:

'What am I here to *do*?'
'Am I *able* to do this?'
'Who am *I* to be doing this?'

For many elders anxieties abound!

Later we shall look at what as an elder you are there on that doorstep to do. We hope we provide help regarding the anxiety underlying the question 'Who am *I* to be doing this?' It is natural for elders who recognise their frailty and who are aware of their high calling as elders, to feel inadequate from time to time. First of all, therefore, we focus on '*How* do I come to be doing this?'

The answer to this question is that you are an elder, and there on the doorstep

because you have been chosen and called to be an elder; and
because you have responded positively to that call.

However, you are also an elder and there on the doorstep, because your call and response are part of a process which began with Creation. Your being where you are is part of the whole story of God's loving communication with humankind—meeting need and inviting a response.

To understand how you come to be doing the work of the eldership, we need not only to look at the practicalities of caring but also the background and context in which our eldership is carried out. We therefore look first at the unfolding story of God's relationship with his Creation.

Your being there is part of the whole story of God's loving communications with humankind.

The human condition

Genesis, chapter 1, tells us that life is no meaningless accident. The universe and life—including humankind—have been brought into existence by God.

Humankind has been made in two forms—male and female. In Genesis, chapter 2, in the story of the Garden, we see Adam naming all the animals. He misses companionship with someone with whom he can relate more closely than he can with the animals. He falls asleep, tired at the end of the day. When he wakes up, there she is—'bone of his bone, flesh of his flesh'—his equal and partner. It must have been a great awakening!

Genesis 1 tells us that humankind is made 'in the image of God'— a religious being able to relate to its Creator; made as the Psalmist says: 'little less than God and crowned with honour and glory'. Humankind is blessed by God and told to be fruitful and to increase to fill the earth and to subdue it, ruling over the fish of the sea, the birds of the air and everything that lives on the earth.

In the story of the Garden, the good creation is called 'Eden' which means 'pleasure'. We are given the beautiful picture of God strolling in the garden in the evening breeze. He is there to talk with his human creation. The whole Bible shows us a God who *communicates*, who wants *dialogue*—a God who relates to his creation, a God who wants to share in its pleasure.

Life's purpose is to enjoy and look after God's good creation— living in harmony with one another and with our God.

The next chapters of Genesis show us how things go wrong in the garden. Our relationship with God is spoiled, as are our relationships with one another, and indeed with Creation itself. We are wanderers on the face of the earth, no longer at home. See Genesis 3:23 and 4:16. We toil with many bad feelings and poor relationships. We seek answers to life's deep questions.

Human beings are religious beings—with the capacity to ask the deep questions about life, questions like:

- Who or what brought the universe and life into being?
- Has life got any ultimate meaning and purpose?
- How ought we to live and behave?
- Why is there so much evil and suffering?
- How can life's wrongs be put right?
- Is death the end of a person?

Life's purpose is to enjoy and look after God's good creation—living in harmony with one another and with our God.

The answers we find to life's religious questions affect greatly our happiness and the happiness of those with whom we share life.

Religious questions, unlike scientific questions, are not open to *proof*. We cannot carry out a controlled experiment to prove whether or not life has any ultimate meaning and purpose. We cannot prove in any moral situation that this or that course of action is right. In every case it is a matter of *belief*. We can believe in a Creator, in God, or we can believe that there is no God, and that life is but the result of some meaningless accident. Either way, *we live by faith*.

Our beliefs about life's religious questions are very important, shaping as they do, many of our choices and the actions which come from these choices.

Our own personal well-being, and that of other people, is also very much related to the answers found to questions like:

- Who am I?
- What kind of person am I?
- Who are these other people around me?
- How do I fit in?

Human beings need to feel that their lives matter, that they belong and fit into something worthwhile.

Our feelings about ourselves and about other people are crucially important. They too shape our attitudes and so our choices and actions.

We human, religious beings need to feel that our lives matter, that we belong, and fit into something worthwhile. We need to feel understood, accepted, valued—loved. Without constructive beliefs and good feelings, leading to a genuine interest in life, we are lost. In the prison of our lostness, and as a result of it, we tend to seek stimulation in violent and destructive ways.

Violence inflicted on other people we see all around us. One group of teenagers explained that the fights they got into 'helped to pass the time'! They had probably never consciously worked out their beliefs, nor analysed their feelings—but they had them and were chained by them.

Self-destructive violence can also be seen all around us. We can see it in children sniffing glue, in teenagers on heroin, in adults consuming rivers of alcohol. The famous film-star George Sanders cited boredom as his reason in his suicide note.

'Most of my patients come to me', said a psychiatrist, 'simply because they are bored'.

The famous psychiatrist, Carl Jung, said of all the patients who consulted him in the second half of life, that is, over 35 years of age, 'not one of them has recovered his *enthusiasm* for living until he has recovered or discovered faith in God'.

'Enthusiasm' is a good word!

Enthusiasm.

God

Following the early chapters of Genesis, which speak to us about God and the human condition, the rest of the Bible is about God's efforts to restore communication with those whom he made in his own image.

A key element in the Old Testament is the belief that God established a special relationship (or covenant) with a people known as Israel. Israel, God hoped, would become a 'light to the Gentiles', that is to the whole world.

We can learn a lot about God from this relationship.

During the Old Testament (= Covenant) times, God spoke to Israel through people called 'prophets', through whom he tried to help his people find the way to enjoy the 'garden'.

God is usually thought of as the *speaker*, but all through the Old Testament God is also shown as the *listener*.

The God who listens . . .

He hears his people's cry:

I hear the people of Israel say in grief . . .

Jeremiah 31:18

He listens to the individual's cry:

In my trouble I called to the Lord, I called to my God for help.
In his temple he heard my voice; he listened to my cry for help.
Psalm 18:6

God's listening is not a sitting back, a mere hearing of the torrents of words spoken in his direction. It is an *active listening* and responding:

I have seen the deep sorrow of my people in Egypt and have heard their pleas for freedom . . . . I have come to deliver them.
Exodus 3:7–8

The great liberating response of God in the Old Testament was The Exodus—the delivering of his people from their chains in Egypt and the opening up of a new, fuller life in Canaan.

. . . and responds.

'How can I give you up,
Israel? How can I abandon
you. My heart will not let
me do it! My love for you is
too strong.'

(Hosea 2:8)

This deliverance was the product of God's active listening and the response of his people. God does not impose his will. If he did the Israelites might have reached Canaan a lot sooner! God listens and responds, inviting response, letting his people be responsible for their response. In chapter 3 we have more to say about this crucially important point.

Turning away from God's way has its consequences. His people learned this to their cost. There is much talk in the Old Testament about God's 'punishments'. We understand this, not in terms of actual punishments—of a divine revenge which says 'I'll show you who's boss!', but as the natural consequence of living contrary to God's design for fullness of life. As there are physical laws, like the law of gravity, so there are moral and spiritual laws which, if broken, have their sad and painful consequences. We may be free to choose what we wish to do. We are not free from the consequences of the choices we make.

Even when his people break their part of the Covenant, God does not give up on them. He continues to listen and to respond.

The faithful in Israel, trusting in the love and care of God, looked to God to establish a new covenant, a new relationship, a new beginning for his people (Jer. 31:31–34).

Jesus

The writers of the New Testament found this new relationship, the new beginning, through Jesus.

> He gave them the cup after the supper, saying 'This cup is God's *new* covenant, sealed with my blood which is poured out for you'.
> Luke 22:20

Jesus is God's response to humankind's continuing separation from him. Through Jesus a new opportunity for dialogue has opened up. We are called to follow Jesus and to join in the dialogue he makes possible. By following Jesus we listen and respond to God and his offer of life in all its original, intended fulness.

The Word of God became much more than words.

> The Word became a human being and, full of grace and truth, lived amongst us.
> John 1:14

'God loved the world so
much that he gave his only
son so that whoever
believes in him may not die
but have eternal life. For
God did not send his son
into the world to be its
judge, but to be its
saviour.'

(John 3:16)

In Jesus God came into our living space to be with us. His listening brought him to respond, to sit where we sit, feel what we feel. His care for us was shown in this total responding. He took our burdens on himself, even to the point of agonising death, to help us put right the things that we do that spoil our life in his 'garden'.

He did not, and does not, wave a magic wand to satisfy all our needs, but through the amazing gift of his loving presence in Christ and his Spirit he offers salvation—freedom, from the chains we place upon ourselves and each other—and he calls us to respond.

In his letter to the Philippians Paul wrote

My God, with all his *abundant wealth* in Christ Jesus, will supply all your needs.

Philippians 4:19

Carl Jung in our age, and Paul long ago, knew that the antidote to boredom, and all our human poverty, is to be found in God—in what we might describe as God's *inexhaustible vitality*. This wealth, vitality, life, has been offered to the world in Jesus.

Christians have much to be enthusiastic about.

What others have said about Jesus and Christian Faith

All day people have been arriving, returning to their native town, the place from which their fathers and their grandfathers had come, going to be taxed.

And so the town was crowded and when night fell it was crowded beyond its capacity. Many homes were crammed with holiday-minded relatives making the most of the required journey, and talking about old times, old hopes.

The inns didn't have a spare bed, mattress or sleeping space. Even the stables behind the inns were occupied by more than animals.

Night thickened and the lines of tethered asses and hobbled camels settled slowly into stillness. Even the dogs, scavenging among the plentiful rubbish of the day, gradually disappeared . . . .

And all was still.

But in one small stable, among the animals, there was a small bustle of urgent, anxious, controlled activity, until to one young mother a son was born.

And this was good news of a new kind—to all sorts of people.

It was good news for the restless minds of wise men from the thoughtful East who knelt before this answer to their questionings, and rejoiced that reason and much learning now united them with shepherds of the field, for whom the heavens were brighter and the path more straight.

Dick Williams

What Christmas means to me is in that baby, and in the man who grew from him, is to be found the meaning of all life.

The Christmas gospel is that what we see in Jesus tells us more about the heart of the universe than anything else. It says that, however it may look on the surface, reality at bottom is like that: love of that quality is the most real, the most powerful thing in the world.

Now that takes a tremendous amount of believing. In fact, it takes so much believing in the world as we know it, that it would be impossible to credit unless in Jesus Christ we have a window through into ultimate reality itself, into God.

And that is what Christmas is claiming—that Jesus of Nazareth is the deepest probe into the meaning of things that we have been given. For in him we reach rock-bottom—that rock of love on which the whole universe is constructed.

What we see on the surface of history in Jesus is what it's like at the centre. That's what in traditional language is meant by the 'divinity of Christ'.

John Robinson

Though even the gospel writers differ from each other in what they see in him (Jesus), just like modern writers they all agree that they find him disturbing because he brings the challenge of purpose.

'Is this', men find themselves asking, 'is this what men ought to be like? Are we all meant to love as he loved, and show the imagination and vision that he showed; are we all meant to find a sort of son-like dependence on God, and the strength and courage and healing power that he found?'

This is the kind of 'wonder' that the New Testament writers hoped to leave us with . . . .

We are left wondering about the kind of life we ought to be living ourselves, whether it is just 'ordinary', or whether it is to rise to something higher, with a queer power for good that we did not even know we possessed.

Harold Loukes

Here is a man who was born in an obscure village, the child of a peasant woman. He worked in a carpenter's shop until he was thirty, and then for three years he was an itinerant preacher. He had no credentials but himself.

While still a young man, the tide of popular opinion turned against him. His friends—the twelve men who had learned so much from him, and had promised him their enduring loyalty—ran away and left him. He went through a mockery of a trial. He was nailed upon a cross between two thieves. When he was dead he was taken down and laid in a borrowed grave through the pity of a friend.

Yet I am well within the mark when I say that all the armies that ever marched, and all the parliaments that ever sat, and all the kings that ever reigned, put together have not affected the life of man upon this earth as has this one solitary life.

Anon

Is it any wonder that the priests realised that between this man and themselves there was no chance but that he or witchcraft should perish? Is it any wonder that the Roman soldiers, confronted and amazed by something soaring over their comprehensions and threatening all their disciplines, should take refuge in wild laughter, and crown him with thorns, and robe him in purple to make a mock Caesar of him?

For to take him seriously was to enter upon a strange and alarming life, to abandon habits, to control instincts and impulses, to essay an incredible happiness.

H G Wells

The crucifixion itself is a victory. Jesus died with his love and his courage unbroken. In that sense he overcame the powers of evil. But it was a bleak victory. Is this the best we can hope for of goodness and love in this world—to die alone in the dark in agony, albeit undefeated?

The resurrection says 'No, it is not.' Here God who had seemed so absent on Good Friday, at last shows his hand. The New Testament never says that Christ rose from the dead. It always says that God raised him from the dead. In the resurrection we know where God stands.

The love Jesus lived for and died for is not a pathetic idyll, out of touch with reality. It *is* reality.

Whatever present appearances may suggest, goodness is stronger than evil. Life is stronger than death. To believe this gives one a new sense of values, and a new perspective on everything.

Here is the conviction that one's struggle after goodness can never be in vain. Here is the ground of hope where the confines of this world give no hope. Here is the hope that illumines even the valley of the shadow of death.

Love is alive for ever, for me.

Wilf Wilkinson

For further reading

Winding Quest, The Heart of the Old Testament, Alan T Dale, Oxford University Press, 1972.

New World, The Heart of the New Testament, Alan T Dale, Oxford University Press, 1967.

Evidence That Demands A Verdict Josh McDowell, Campus Crusade For Christ, 1973.

Portrait of Jesus, Alan T Dale, Oxford University Press, 1979.

Essentials, David L Edwards, and John Stott, Hodder & Stoughton, 1988.

Jesus Then and Now, David Watson, Lion, 1983.

You come to be on that doorstep because of God and what, through Jesus, he has done for all humankind. You are there because of Jesus and the Christian Church which came into being soon after his death and resurrection.

The Christian Church

'Go then to all peoples everywhere and make them my disciples . . . I will be with you always.'
(Matthew 20:19ff)

Jesus' first followers walked many a mile with him as he healed the sick and strove to set people free from their chains. They shared many a dangerous moment with him as he shared his faith, his enthusiasm for life and the kingdom of God. They watched his physical body cruelly beaten and then broken on a cross. Confusion and utter despair followed this sight but soon they came to experience and know that his life-giving ministry had not come to an end. They knew he wanted them to share his *continuing ministry*.

The Spirit-filled transformation in their lives was amazing. They became convinced of his call to them to go to all the inhabitants of God's 'garden' and of his promise to be with them in their faith-sharing.

And so an enthusiastic new movement came into being—the Christian Church—a people with a purpose (a mission) to share with the world:

- New eyes with which to see.
- New ears with which to listen.
- New minds to understand life.
- New hearts to love and trust and risk.

The New Testament often describes the Church as 'the body of Christ'—an awesome term when we think of what Jesus' physical body had to endure. Sharing Christian beliefs and values in a society which thinks differently can be very dangerous. It was certainly so in the early centuries of the Church as the following account shows.

A Roman provincial governor decided that his capital should have a coliseum like the one in Rome. He employed a Greek architect to design and supervise the construction. When the building was completed an opening ceremony was held. At its climax some Christians were led into the arena. The audience excitedly awaited the opening of the gates for the wild animals that could be heard.

When the architect realised what was about to happen, he left his prominent seat and jumped down into the arena.

'Come back', called the governor.

'I belong here', replied the architect, 'for I am a Christian.'

'But you are my friend. I don't want you to be killed', said the governor.

'And you are my friend' said the architect, 'but these people are my brothers and sisters. If they die, I die with them.'

That story also shows that, central to their life as his Church was the love and care and support Jesus asked his followers to have for one another (John 15:5–17).

The New Testament, with its great honesty, records the difficulties the early Christian communities had in this regard. Its writers stress again and again the importance of love for one another. Without love, Paul said, we are nothing. *To a great extent our Christian credibility depends upon the love we demonstrate.*

Ministry

In Ephesians, chapter 4, at the end of verse 8, the writer talks about Jesus giving gifts to his people. At verse 11, in the Authorised Version of the Bible, we read:

> And he gave some, apostles; and some prophets; and some, evangelists; and some, pastors and teachers;

and in verse 12:

> *for* the perfecting of the saints,
> *for* the work of the ministry,
> *for* the edifying of the body of Christ.

It appears from this that gifts and talents are given to a variety of what we might call 'specialists' who have the purpose of *'perfecting'*, *'ministering'* to, and *'edifying'* the members of the Church. This is a very common way in which people have viewed, and still view, the role of those we call 'the ministers'.

The Authorised Version dates from 1611. You will notice the translators' love of commas and semi-colons. The New Testament was first written in Greek, which did not use commas and semi-colons. One of the Authorised Version's commas is misplaced.

In the original Greek of verse 12 the first 'for' is the Greek word *'pros'* which means 'for'. The second and third 'for' in the Greek are *'eis'* which means 'unto'. Verse 12 should therefore read:

> for the perfecting of the saints
> unto the work of ministry,
> unto the edifying of the body of Christ.

The New English Bible corrects the error and updates the language. It tells us that the role of the 'specialists' is:

> to equip God's people
> for work in his service
> to the building up of the body of Christ.

The Good News translation says:

> He did this to prepare all God's people for the work of Christian service, in order to build up the body of Christ.

Clearly the New Testament is telling us that gifts or talents are given to various 'specialists' to enable every member to play his or her part in the shared ministry (= service) of all God's people. Everyone who belongs to God's Church is part of a shared ministry of caring for each other *and* of caring for the world.

Everyone who belongs to God's Church is part of a shared ministry.

The local congregation

The local congregation is part of the basic unit of the Church in every generation.

A vital element in the life of the Church, from New Testament times to the present day, in all the different denominations and forms of church organisation, has been the local congregation. We can think of it as the *basic unit* of the Church in every generation. The effectiveness of the Christian movement is very dependent upon the quality of the lifestyle of its congregations. It therefore depends very much upon the quality of leadership provided and whether or not it develops the shared ministry spoken about on p.20. The unholy alliance of church members who wait to be ministered to and leaders who seek to do all the ministering has devitalised and deskilled many a congregation!

In the New Testament we see a variety of patterns of organisation as the early Church grew and tried to carry out its shared ministry through its local congregations. Different forms of Church government have emerged and exist today. Each of the different denominations of the Church belongs to one or other of the following forms:

Presbyterian   Episcopal   Congregational

Since the Church is a living organism changes are always taking place. There can be differences even within the same tradition. We confine ourselves to the following simple statement of the Presbyterian form which is based on a system of courts.

The Presbyterian tradition

- *The Session*: the lowest court, made up of the minister and the elders of a local congregation. The Session has the responsibility of leading its congregation's ministry.

- *The Presbytery*: this court consists of the minister and one elder of each congregation in a given geographical area. It is responsible for overseeing the life of these congregations.

- *The Synod*: this court is made up of representatives (ministers and elders in equal numbers) of each Presbytery in a given geographical area. It handles various matters dealing with Presbyteries and their congregations.

- *The General Assembly*: the supreme court, made up of ministers and elders, again in equal numbers, appointed by Presbyteries from their congregations on a rota basis.

The Session may be described as the lowest court in that it is subject to the higher courts. It may, however, be viewed as the most important one because of its leadership of the basic unit, the local congregation. The elders of a Session are *ordained*, solemnly set apart, for this crucial purpose.

The companion handbook for elders, *Leading God's People*, deals with the Session's leadership task, as outlined in the diagram opposite. In *Caring for God's People* we concentrate on the Christian fellowship/pastoral care circle.

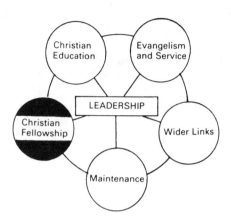

The district elder

Many Presbyterian branches of the Church have developed a pastoral dimension to the role of their elders. For example, in 1648 the General Assembly of the Church of Scotland resolved that every elder should have a district, a number of families 'to watch over'. This was instituted at the time as one of the remedies for 'profaneness' and had to do with discipline within the local congregation.

> The office of the Elder is severally and conjunctly to watch over the flock committed to their charge, both publicly and privately, that no corruption of religion or manners enter therein.
>
> Cox's *Practice and Procedure in the Church of Scotland*

Because the witness of the local congregation is so very important, discipline is a serious matter. Caring for God's people is, however, a very much wider thing.

To each elder of the Church of Scotland:

> there is normally assigned a district for the oversight of which he (the Elder) is responsible. He should assist the Minister in the care of the sick, the aged and the needy, and in encouraging those outside the Church to respond to the Gospel, and to enter the fellowship of the Church.
>
> Pardovan's *Collection*

time for a new image of the elder

In the United Reformed Church elders are given a group to care for—a number of members of the congregation. The third of the duties of the URC elders' meeting reads as follows:

> To ensure the pastoral care of the congregation, in which the minister is joined by Elders having particular responsibility for groups of members.

In *Being an Elder Today—in the United Reformed Church* elders are described as being:

> The chosen and appointed agents of pastoral care, in partnership with the Minister.

This idea of *partnership* is preferable to that of assistant. The district elder has an important ministry in his or her own right. To care for the sick, the aged, the needy (a wide term that!) and to encourage those 'outside' to discover our faith is quite a calling. It should, of course, be viewed within the context of the shared ministry of all the members of the congregation.

The writer of an early twentieth-century Australian publication says to the district elder:

> It is better that the children tug your coat, than that they should run to the remotest corner of the yard at your appearing.

There will be many tugs for those who care for God's people.

For further reading

History of Christianity, Jim Dowley, Lion 1977.

Church of Scotland

A Guide to Congregational Affairs, Andrew Herron, The Saint Andrew Press, 1978.
A Guide to the General Assembly of the Church of Scotland, Andrew Herron, The Saint Andrew Press, 1976.
A Guide to the Presbytery, Andrew Herron, The Saint Andrew Press, 1983.
Our Church, RD Kernohan, The Saint Andrew Press, 1985.
Leading God's People, Stewart G Matthew and Kenneth Scott, The Saint Andrew Press, 1986.
God's Scotland: The Story of Scottish Christian Religion, Anne Pagan, Mainstream, 1988.

PAMPHLETS
'The Elder in the Church Today', D.F. Anderson, The Saint Andrew Press.
'The Elder and the Sacraments', D.F. Anderson, The Saint Andrew Press.
'The Office of Elder in the Church of Scotland', The Saint Andrew Press.

FRONTLINE MATERIALS: CHURCH OF SCOTLAND EDUCATION DEPT
'Approaching Ordination to the Eldership' (Frontline code B4).
'The Development of the Eldership' (Frontline code A21).

FRONTLINE TARGET PACK
'For Members of the Kirk Session' (includes above B4 article).

Presbyterian Church in Ireland

'Training Course for Elders', Committee on Christian Training.
'Choosing New Elders', Board of Evangelism and Christian Training.
The History of the Church: Our Presbyterian Heritage, Finlay Holmes, Publications Committee.
Henry Cooke, Finlay Holmes, Christian Journals Ltd.

United Reformed Church

'Being an Elder in the United Reform Church', Stephen H Mayor, United Reformed Church.
'Tell Me About the URC', John H Taylor, United Reformed Church.

FAITH AND LIFE DEPARTMENT LEAFLETS
'Leadership in the Church'
'Choosing our Elders'
'An Elder? Who? Me?'

For thinking through

Identify what has led you to where you are now in your eldership. Think back as far as you can and note the people, influences, convictions, doubts, feelings and beliefs which have contributed:

- to your becoming an elder;
- to your development as an elder.

Share with your fellow-elders what you wish of what you have discovered.

Two questions to be answered by yourself and the answers shared with your fellow-elders:

- Why am I an elder? (This is not about why you became an elder but why you are one at this present time.)
- What do I feel about being an elder? (This is not about thoughts but feelings such as joy, frustration, anger, sadness, boredom, etc.)

Eldership can be seen in the light of 'God's offer of faith, love, enthusiasm, vitality through Jesus'?

- What other words would you use to describe God's offer?
- In what ways do you see your eldership in the light of 'the importance to every human being of constructive beliefs, good feelings and a genuine interest in life'?

2 Getting started

Your primary purpose is to develop a caring relationship.

The door opens. As an elder you have no right of entry. Hopefully you will be recognised and welcomed in.

You may have visited this household many times before. This may be your first visit. It may be a pre-communion visit if that is part of your congregation's tradition. Your visit may be part of some visiting programme that the elders are carrying out. You may be there to enlist help, pass on information, seek the views of your members about something. You may be there because of some event, happy or sad, in the life of those who live beyond this doorstep.

Whatever the reason, the primary purpose of your being there is to develop a caring relationship with the people of your district.

Some practical guidelines

Notebook

It is useful for elders to have a private notebook containing helpful information about the people in their care.

- names, relationships occupations, interests, skills;
- church involvements (past and present);
- special events *eg* birthdays, anniversaries, bereavements;
- dates visited.
- matters for referral *eg* the name of a young person whom the Bible class leader might contact.

Private notebooks must, of course, be private.

For a new elder, or one taking over a new district, it is helpful if, before setting out, some basic information is gathered about the people to be visited. Time could be usefully spent with the minister or the previous elder if there was one, in this regard. There may be sensitive information which should be given to avoid the making of needless, and perhaps embarrassing or hurtful mistakes, *eg* asking a woman who is separated from her husband 'Is your husband out?'

It is prudent to avoid seeking, or being given, any opinions and judgements about people. It is better to form first one's own impressions. Where one elder has developed a good relationship, another elder may find it more difficult, and vice versa. People are different and respond to each other differently. If it seems important to do so impressions can be checked out with the minister or previous elder once the relationship has been established.

Timing visits

For most elders visiting is likely to be done in the evenings, if for no other reason than that the elder and/or the people being visited are at work during the day.

Some visits may have to be made earlier in the day, *eg* to an elderly person who does not like to open their door after dark, particularly in the winter months. Meal times are not, as a rule, good times to call, nor is the time of the favourite TV 'soap'.

For young families the early evening, with bathtimes and homework, may not be convenient—though times will have to be found to meet with the children of the household. You are *their* elder as well! For other people, *eg* late shift workers, early bedders, the late evening would not be an appropriate time to call. The weekend may have to be used for some visits.

The timing of visits requires sensitivity and its appropriateness needs to be checked out. A cordial welcome does not necessarily mean that a good time has been chosen. For a whole host of reasons it may not always be easy for somebody to respond positively to our request to be allowed to come in. There are times, when, with the best will in the world, it is not convenient for our best friend to call without warning!

If you do arrive at an inconvenient time you can offer to return at a more suitable time. An arrangement to do so could perhaps be made there and then. Some elders give advance notice by delivering a visiting card stating when they will call. Some elders use the telephone to arrange agreed times. This is courteous. It is, of course, then very important to keep the appointment or, if absolutely necessary, to make contact to explain that your plans have had to be changed.

The people you visit should also have your address and telephone number in case they want to contact you. This information could be

on your visiting card. A visiting card is also useful to leave when you have called and got a locked door. It lets people know you did call.

As you get to know the people you will be better able to plan your visits. Developing a caring relationship includes sensitive planning of visits.

Elders often express frustration about never getting across some doorsteps. With better planning and preparation the problem might be reduced. It is, of course, a strange church household that posts a 'No entry' sign to its elder. The minister may be able to help, perhaps by discussing the situation with the family or perhaps by visiting with the elder. There may have been some hurt or misunderstanding in the past, real or imagined, which is causing the discourtesy.

Where there is no such reason the member or family may have to become the concern of the whole Session in terms of what is called 'discipline'. There is much for a Session to do regarding the 'body-life' of its congregation (see p 117) if there are many homes barred to its elders. It had better look first to itself—to how its elders plan their visits and to the quality and meaningfulness of the visiting which is being done. It might find useful what is said later about a more developed pastoral strategy (see chapter 8).

In some Presbyterian denominations the elder's visit has been very much linked to the pre-communion season and so to the delivering of communion cards. This may be part of the elder's pastoral care—the invitation to the sacrament—but in our opinion it must not be equated with pastoral care. The card, and so the visit, can be seen, not as an invitation, but as a summons! When someone says to an elder 'Oh, its that time again' it is unlikely that they view the visit as a demonstration of a genuine interest in them. Perhaps this is one reason why getting the TV switched off can be difficult!

Length of visit

In the planning of your visits it is wise, for your own sake, as well as the sake of those whom you hope to visit, not to attempt to make too many visits to too many different people in any given period of time.

People need to feel that they matter and have not just been fitted in to a busy schedule (*eg* a pre-communion round-up—'I can't stay long. I have a lot of calls to get through'!)

Your visits are not to be rushed. *Caring and relationship-building take time*. On the other hand your visits are not to be prolonged beyond the point of usefulness and enjoyment. No precise guidance

Visiting in happy times

Elder Mrs Stewart visits the Ross family whose daughter Elizabeth has won first prize in a short-story competition run by a national magazine for teenagers.

Mrs R: (bringing Mrs S into the living room. Elizabeth is there) Come in . . . Elizabeth, it's Mrs Stewart!

Mrs S: Hello Elizabeth.

Elizabeth: Hello there Mrs Stewart. Dad's upstairs having a bath. Come and have a seat.

Mrs S: Well, its really you I've come to see . . . I've just been reading about you in the evening paper, I wanted to say congratulations about winning that short-story competition.

Elizabeth: Thanks . . . it's really nice of you to come round. Its exciting . . . I've to go to London to get my prize . . . it's great. They're taking me on a tour of the magazine's offices, then on to see the magazine getting printed and *then* on to the Savoy for lunch!

Mrs S: That sounds wonderful (turns to Mrs R) you must be very proud of her.

Mrs R: Oh yes . . . you see she's always wanted to write and this is a great boost for her.

Mrs S: (to Elizabeth) So when do we get to see your story?

Elizabeth: It's in next month's magazine (she laughs) I've told so many people that the newsagent will have to double his order!

Mrs S: I must make sure and order *my* copy then . . . . Tell me, did it take you long to write?

Elizabeth: Well, by the time I'd chopped and changed it—about three weeks. It got really frustrating at times . . . I never dreamed I'd get a prize at all . . . never mind first prize!

Mrs S: Well, I hope you have a great time in London, you certainly deserve it after all your hard work. (She gets up and gets ready to leave).

Mrs R: Thanks for calling . . . we both appreciate you taking such an interest. (Elizabeth opens the door for her)

Mrs S: Not at all. My pleasure! Well, I'll see you both soon, say hello to Mr Ross for me, Cheerio!

Taken from video cassette 'Training in Eldership': "Pastoral Care"

can, we think, be given about the length of any visit. Who knows what may be discovered, or may surface, on any visit beyond the doorstep?

You may find some members more welcoming and enjoyable to

For thinking through

Share with fellow-elders how you:

- Use a notebook.
- Time your visits.
- Deal with someone who does not invite you in.
- Cope with a television which is left on.
- Determine the length of a visit.

Share with each other experiences of visiting members just to celebrate something good that has happened in a home.

- What did it require of you?
- What did you get from these visits?

Share what you think about the frequency of visiting.

As a rough guide to building a good relationship, plan to visit quarterly *and* on some of these 'special occasions'.

be with. It would be surprising if you didn't. The temptation can come to us to spend more time with them.

Frequency of visits

An elderly and lonely person might welcome a weekly visit. It is unlikely that you could visit many people on such a regular basis. Most people would feel a visit from you every week or two to be an imposition. Caring persons do not impose themselves on other people.

On the other hand, a visit once or twice a year may require the ice to be broken each time. If someone in the family is out it could be a year or more since last you talked to them. Such visits are not easily recognised as good pastoral care, nor do they help much in the developing of caring relationships. They run the risk of becoming what a church member once described as 'meaningless interruptions'!

> Every new situation in a family's life—birth, marriage, death, sickness, leaving school, a change of job—is an opportunity for forging another link in the chain of trust and understanding between elder and member.
>
> David Anderson

In a number of these 'special occasions' it is good for the district elder to be associated with the minister, *eg* sharing together a call to prepare for a wedding, a baptism, a funeral. When a child is being baptised the child's elder can stand alongside the parents who are taking vows. When, at a funeral, the elder is invited to take a coffin cord the old hymn comes to mind—'Blest be the tie that binds our hearts in Christian love'.

We would wish to emphasise the importance of visiting in happy times. On p 28 there is an account of a brief visit by an elder to mark a happy occasion. The value of that visit was no doubt far in excess of the time and effort it took. To make such a visit does, of course, require a good knowledge of the people you visit. It you build up a good relationship in the happy times, you may be better able, and more welcome, to share in the difficult times.

As a rough guide to building a good relationship, plan to visit quarterly *and* on some of these 'special occasions'.

Communication

An important part of building a good relationship is the development of good communication.

Communication is often seen as one person telling another person about something, *eg* the date of the next communion, some congregational event, the congregation's need for more money. We begin to look at this differently when we grasp that the word 'communication' has the same basic meaning as the words 'community' and 'communion'. It has to do with *having something in common* and with *sharing*. It has to do with developing a relationship; with people sharing who they are, what they think, feel and believe; being open to each other.

Good communication is open, caring dialogue, enriching both the visitor and the visited. Our openness invites and encourages others to be open. *Openness is essential to good communication which is basic to pastoral care.*

The next chapter expands on this. For the moment your attention is drawn to John Powell's* levels of communication and to some common blocks to open, caring communication.

Levels of communication

1 *Cliché:* This is the most basic level, dealing with ordinary things in an everyday way. At this level we are opening a conversation, getting to know someone, or keeping the conversation at a very safe level. We may be talking about the weather, the prices in the shops, football or one of a number of subjects which oil the wheels of communication.

2 *Others:* Having tested the water at the cliché level, we may go on to talk about other people. We may talk about someone who is significant to us, *eg* a member of the family, a neighbour, the minister, a TV personality. We may talk about someone else who is less significant. We may give an unbiased account of their behaviour or we may gossip about them. We may be speaking in general terms about what everybody thinks or does. What we are not doing at this level is sharing much about ourselves.

3 *Thoughts:* If we choose to move on to this level we begin to share something of ourselves, by talking about what goes on in our heads. This may include our opinions, judgements or beliefs. At

this level we feel more vulnerable than we do on either of the previous levels because the response to what we are sharing is unknown.

4 *Feelings:* When we share our feelings we feel more vulnerable because it is as if we are handing ourselves over to others. All sorts of questions come into our minds about what others will think, or if they will continue to value and love us, as well as all kinds of thoughts about not sharing our feelings, not letting our hearts rule our heads. We may be inhibited from sharing feelings which some people believe are wrong. However, the benefits of being able to describe and share our feelings to another person can be immense.

It can be especially difficult to share a feeling with the person about whom you have the feeling. This can be just as true for feelings such as joy and love as it is for feelings like anger or fear. It is necessary for us all to have someone with whom we can share at this level because the feelings, if they remain bottled up, can blow the cork in an explosive way or else they can fester away under the surface for years—souring a person's life and relationships. How often elders discover evidence that small hurts from the past can grow and grow over the years until there is a wide gulf between one individual and another or between a family and the church.

5 *Peak:* If we have shared at the other levels, gradually trusting the other person with more of ourselves, we have prepared the way for communication of complete openness and honesty.

We are not on this level often, nor do we stay on it for long, but we do know when we are there. Something 'clicks' between us and another person. We know we are 'on the same wavelength'. We feel understood, accepted and even loved. The communication may be largely non-verbal.

A relationship usually begins at the first level and as it progresses and people become comfortable with each other, it moves on to the next level, and so on. It can stay at any level and can even come back down from one level to another—temporarily or permanently. It is important to accept that people move from one level to another at different speeds. They may miss out a level or spend a very brief time on it.

It is important to recognise on which level we are prepared to be with another person, and they with us. Caring communication can only take place on the level at which both parties feel at ease. When people operate at different levels much frustration can be experienced. When each responds at the appropriate level the other is invited to move to a higher level and both experience a deepening relationship.

As elders we may wish to communicate on a different level from the person we are visiting, *eg* the other person may wish to stay at the cliché (superficial) level, while we may wish to go beyond chit-chat. It is important that we begin where the other person feels comfortable.

We may experience the temptation to keep things at the cliché level in case the other person leads us into deep waters. If we refuse to operate at the other levels our visits may well be described as 'meaningless interruptions'!

To develop a caring relationship requires moving beyond the superficial. It is not caring to force or manipulate other people, but we can, by our attitude and our response to them, invite them to move on to other levels. This they will do in their own time as they come to accept, feel comfortable with, and trust us. We may know ourselves to be trustworthy. The people we visit have to discover this for themselves. For some, because of past experiences in other situations, this may take some time. Only our patient, caring, openness and acceptance of them will invite them to try communicating with us on a higher level.

This idea of five levels of communication is not intended to inhibit spontaneity or our own natural gifts of communication, but to help us to be more aware of ourselves and others and so to be more caring in our response to the needs we all have.

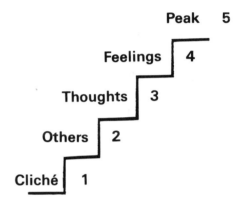

Blocks to communication

In all our relationships there are many ways in which we can hinder, or even put an end to, caring communication. In his book, *The Miracle of Dialogue*, Reuel Howe lists five blocks to communication

1 Images

James Baldwin says in *Nobody Knows My Name*: 'As negroes we find that people do not address us because of who we are, but address the image they have of us. You don't know me. You just know who you think I am.'

In order to communicate with others, we need to listen to who they really are and to what is actually going on inside them.

For thinking through

Think of the various people whom you visit.

- Can you identify examples of the five levels of communication in the relationships you have with them?
- Are there any with whom you are on a level which is different from the one on which they are?
- What effect does that have on your relationship?
- Are there any people with whom you wish to change level? How would they feel about that?

Think of an experience of 'peak' communication you have had.

Using your imagination, get back into the experience.

- What was good for you?
- What did the other person(s) involved gain from your shared experience?
- What did you learn from that experience that could help you in other situations?

NB If any of the above is shared with other elders great care must be taken regarding confidentiality.

Otherwise we are not communicating with the real person, but rather with an image of the person which we have in our head.

It is important to remember that other people will similarly have their images of us. We need therefore to be open with other people, helping them to correct or discard the images in their heads. *Then, and only then, can real people listen and respond to real people.*

2 Words

Words are, at best, inadequate means of communication. They mean different things to different people. They can have more than one meaning and can carry more than one message. Their meaning can change with changing tones of voice.

Words can be used to confuse or put down the less articulate. They can be used as weapons. They can be hidden behind. We can hide behind our own words. We can choose only to listen and to respond to the words of another person and ignore what that person is communicating by other means (p 39f).

Words, for a variety of reasons, can block communication. *On the other hand the careful and caring use of words can give expression to the deeper levels of communication.*

3 Contrary purposes

There will be little communication if one person's attitude is that he is going to say what he has to say, come what may and regardless of the other person and their expectations. There is rarely much communication between two people both of whom are determined to persuade the other person of the rightness of their own point of view, and the wrongness of the other person's position. Two people operating on different levels mentioned on pp 30f will communicate little.

In situations like these there is little real *dialogue*. What is taking place is better described as two *monologues*. Each participant, instead of listening, is thinking up what to say next when the other person pauses to draw breath!

We need to be clear about our purpose, be ready to share it, and, if necessary, to divide the available time amongst all concerned. We may have to be prepared to change levels.

4 Anxiety

There are different causes of anxiety in communicating with other people. We may be anxious about our performance. Are we saying the right words, doing the right thing, responding appropriately to the situation? We may be anxious about what the other person may say or do, about their attitude towards us, about living up to their expectations. We can, of course, be anxious about landing in a situation in which we feel out of our depth and unable to cope.

Anxiety is about how we shall survive and whether or not we shall continue to be welcomed and appreciated.

If we feel anxious there will be a block in our communication. We also need to recognise that other people may feel anxious with us—even though we cannot imagine why anyone should feel like that with us! *To unblock the communication anxiety has to be faced up to and worked through.*

To unblock communication, anxiety has to be worked through.

5 Defensiveness

If we view other people as a potential threat we are likely to get defensive. We may defend ourselves in a number of ways—by justifying, blaming, withdrawing inside ourselves or actually moving away. Responses like these clearly block communication.

Blocking devices

We would draw your attention to some other responses which *are blocking devices*:

- *Judging*: When someone is sharing something with us we sometimes respond with a criticism, a snap judgement telling the person what they should or should not have said or done, should or should not be feeling.

  We may give an unnecessary and unasked for diagnosis or evaluation: 'I know what your problem is and I just want to tell you.' Even if asked for, and even if apparently accepted, such a response may well block further communication.
- *Solving*: Solving other people's problems is a great temptation, especially perhaps for those of us to whom has been entrusted the care of people. We may hear ourselves saying, after a remarkably short time of listening, 'If I were you I would

It is only by listening and responding that we communicate care.

. . .'. We may even go further by saying 'What you have got to do is . . .'. While rescuing people who are drowning by throwing them a lifebelt is a positive thing to do, rescuing people who do not need to be rescued is a negative, discounting response to their need. We do this when we solve, or attempt to solve, a person's problem for them. We may tell them to pull themselves together, to dry their eyes or to undertake some particular course of action—as if they were incapable of working out their own solution. The temptation to do this is to be resisted in favour of supporting them as they struggle to do their own solving.

- *Avoiding*: Rather than judging or solving we may choose to ignore a difficult situation by diverting the conversation along other lines. We can do this by saying—'That reminds me of what happened to me last week when . . .' or 'I'd love to hear more about that but I'm afraid I haven't the time.' Here endeth communication!

A combination of judging, solving and avoiding, such as 'You should not feel angry about that. Go and pray about it' is virtually certain to put an end to further communication, at the time and in the future.

The same result may be achieved by the use of logical argument in such a way as to ignore the other person's *feelings*. To say 'I know Mr Smith did not mean it like that because he believes . . . and he has said to me . . . and therefore if you . . .' may be helpful but only if the feelings of the person spoken to have first been acknowledged and been sensitively paid attention to.

- Discounting: In all blocking of communication there is an element of discounting—the discounting of our own or other people's abilities and/or feelings, or the discounting of the importance of a problem or situation.

In the next chapter we shall expand on these guidelines to developing good communications as we look at two keys which open communication and keep it unblocked. These keys are *listening* and *responding*. It is only through disciplined use of these that we communicate care.

We end this 'Getting started' chapter with a brief word about prayer—a topic we return to in chapter 4.

Before making any arrangements to visit, and before setting out, you might consider spending some time—perhaps with the help of your notebook—visualising the individual people in your district (including the children and any family members who do not belong to the church), remembering them before God in prayer.

> The sure test of the concern of an elder for his people will be the urgency with which he brings them before the throne of Grace. Some will remember one family by name every day, others will try to cover all the families once per week. Methods may vary, but the beginning of any efforts to serve the members of a district in God's name must be knowing them in God's presence.
>
> George Wilkie

You can create a space for yourself to talk with God about them *and* to listen to what God may have to say to you about them. You may discover that there is a particular person or family whom God wants you to be with. There may be a joy or sorrow, unknown to you, but not to God, in which God wants you to share. God is not to be discounted!

In your planning you need to leave room for God's planning. If you do, you may hear people say 'You must have known that . . .' or 'I was hoping you would call . . .' or 'You have come at just the right time.'

For further reading

Why am I Afraid to Love?, John Powell, Fontana, 1967.
Why Am I Afraid to Tell You Who I Am? John Powell, Fontana, 1969.
Restoring the Image: *An Introduction to Christian Caring and Counselling*, Roger Hurding, Paternoster Press, 1980.
Pastoral Care for Lay People, Frank Wright, Student Christian Movement, 1982.
Rediscovering Pastoral Care, Alastair V Campbell, Darton, Longman and Todd, 1981.

For thinking through

Some of the ideas on pp 32ff are easier to read than to recognise in practice.

If you have a conversation in the next two or three days which does not go as well as you would have liked, report it on a grid like the following.

	I blocked communication by	My communication was blocked by
Images		
Words		
Contrary purposes		
Anxiety		
Defensiveness		
Judging		
Solving		
Avoiding		

Spend some time after each incident working out how you could have done it differently.

Think of an occasion when you felt discounted by someone else.

What was being discounted?

- You as a person?
- Your abilities?
- Your feelings?
- Your problem or its importance?

What were your feelings?

How was the communication between you and the other person affected?

3 Learning to care

You are invited into the house. On the walk from the front door to the living room various questions may go through your mind:

- Who am I going to meet here?
- How will they respond to me?
- What might I have to face?
- Will I be able to cope?
- What if I get out of my depth?

Questions like these point to the anxiety you may, not unnaturally, be feeling. It is helpful to have other questions firmly in mind:

- What is happening in the life of this family?
- What are their needs, questions, joys, difficulties?
- What are they feeling good or bad about?

Questions like these help to *focus* attention on the people you are visiting rather than on your own anxieties. They will help you to begin to *listen*. They could form part of your prayer as you set out on your visits, and certainly as you walk up the path to knock on the door.

Listening: the basic caring skill

Since far more time is spent on listening than on reading, writing or arithmetic, it is surprising that there is little training in listening skills given at school.

Listening is a skill which we all have, but which needs to be developed. Researchers have found that in normal conversation people tend to remember, immediately after listening, only about 50 per cent of what they have heard. Within eight hours a further 33 to 50 per cent is forgotten.

Listening is more than hearing.

A child in a classroom may hear the words the teacher is speaking

Changing the focus.

Listening is more than hearing.

but because the words are uninteresting, or less interesting than what is going on outside the window, the teacher may say quite correctly: 'You are not listening to me!'

Hearing is the means by which sensations in the ear are transmitted to the brain. Listening includes hearing. It also involves the interpretation and understanding of the significance of what is being heard.

Listening is active. Listening is the giving of concentrated, disciplined attention. It is hearing and attempting to discover the meaning and significance of what is being heard.

People do not feel cared for when they are not being listened to or when they are not sure if they are being listened to.

There are two roots to the meaning of the word listen: 'to hear' and 'to wait in suspense'. In the everyday world we hear much but we do not often listen at a deep level.

Active, or creative, listening is waiting expectantly and with an openness to what is being said, while one's own thoughts, opinions, judgements and anxieties are suspended. And that can take practice! The priority is to listen and all the listener's energy and attention are channelled in that direction.

Listening pays attention to—the *words* used, the *way* they are used, and the *spaces* and *silences* between the words. When we are listening we also hear what is not being said!

Listening also pays attention to people's *feelings*.

Feelings are often openly expressed and can be clearly heard: 'I feel blazing mad!' 'I'm so fed up'. Emotive, abusive, exaggerated and coarse words and expressions may be used. It is important to note the intensity of the feeling which is being expressed. Sometimes we have to listen very hard because a feeling may be strongly held though not strongly expressed. Sometimes, indeed often, we try to conceal our feelings. Sometimes feelings are masked. A person may appear angry when in fact they feel despairing. Tears can mask a deep anger. The person wearing the mask may not be fully aware of their deeper feelings but these can be 'heard' by the attentive listener.

Listening involves *eyes* as well as ears. Feelings which are not being expressed in words, or even in tone of voice, are often being expressed by *the language of the body*. The body talks! Anger can be seen in the clenched fist or jaw. Depression can be seen in the listless eyes or bowed head. Tension reveals itself in the drumming of fingers or the constant shifting of position.

Sometimes what is heard with the eyes is different from what is heard with the ears. A person may be shifting in their seat and fidgeting with their hands while saying 'Thank you for coming to visit me. I always feel relaxed with you.' *Two different sets of messages are being given*. It is important to hear both, and particularly the body message. A person may be able to control how they put their thoughts into words. It can be harder to control what the body is saying. Our feelings can be shown in spite of ourselves and sometimes we are not aware of the fact.

SESSION MATTERS

Getting the message

I knew on Saturday it would be Frank's birthday. Frank was an elder. He used to call me his 'boy minister', with I think no disrespect intended. After all, half a century separated us in age at the time.

On the Saturday afternoon I visited Frank. For quite a time we sat at his fireside and talked about this and that. It was pleasant. I remember that someone else called in to wish him a happy birthday. After the person had gone we talked on for a bit and then I began to take my leave.

As I was getting up I sensed that Frank had something to say. I can't remember what he said. Perhaps he didn't remember what he said. Perhaps he didn't say anything, but somehow I knew he had something else to say. As I slowly eased myself back down in the chair the old man started to speak and I knew that the visit, the real meeting, was about to begin. On his 80th birthday I got the story of his life—his joys and sorrows, the pleasures and disappointments he had experienced. It was heartwarming.

Our visits as elders shouldn't be controlled by Communion card delivery. Just as we look to our fellow-members for support on important church occasions, so we should pay attention to them at their times of importance—and not just the times of difficulty, also the times of celebration and the landmarks like my friend Frank's 80th birthday.

People need attention. It is often said that one of the most caring things we can do for another person is really to listen to them.

Jesus said, tellingly. 'He who has ears to hear, let him hear.' We have to learn to hear what is said, not what we think is going to be said, but what is actually being said. It can be helpful to feed back to the person what he or she has said so that we know we heard accurately and the person knows himself/herself truly heard. And we need to hear what is not being said, or being half-said, or being said to camouflage the real message. Listening is an art!

Jesus also said, 'He who has eyes to see, let him see.'

Listening with our eyes is important. The way people (including ourselves!) sit, stand, massage imaginary pains, avert our eyes, furrow our brow, and much else—'body language' as it is now called—all speak to us and help us, if we have the eyes to see, to understand each other.

I am grateful that that Saturday afternoon I got the message, the plea, the invitation to listen.

For thinking through

Identify a recent situation in which you felt someone did not really listen to you.

- What did the person *do* to communicate this to you?

Share your experiences.

Identify a recent situation in which you felt someone did really listen to you

- What did the person *do* to communicate this to you?
- What was it about that listening which helped you?

Share your experiences.

Identify a person you visit, to whom you find it difficult to listen, and apply what you have learned about listening from your discussion together.

At a later date, share your experiences

Listening communicates an attitude of openness to the other person: of genuine acceptance, of caring, encouraging the other person to feel safe and to be able to share what they want to share.

Listening is . . .

One friend, one person who is truly understanding, who takes the trouble to listen to us as we consider our problems, can change our whole outlook on the world.

Dr Elton Mayo

My friends listen to what I say, but my parents only hear me talk.

a teenager

One of the primary tasks of a listener is to stay out of the other's way so the listener can discover how the speaker views the situation.

Robert Bolton

The beginning of wisdom is silence. The second stage is listening.

Hebrew sage

Drawing on my fine command of language—I said nothing.

Robert Buckley

To be able to really listen, one should abandon, or put aside all prejudices . . . . When you are in a receptive frame of mind things can be easily understood . . . . But, unfortunately, most of us listen through a screen of resistance. We are screened with prejudices, whether religious or spiritual, psychological or scientific, or with daily worries, desires and fears. And, with those fears for a screen, we listen. Therefore we listen really to our own noise, our own sound, not to what is being said.

Krishnamurtri

For thinking through

Invite two elders to read the parts of Mrs Henry and Mr James in the following script and after the reading to share what they feel about the role each has played.

Mr James is an elder who has called to visit Mrs Henry. The visit is a normal routine call which is part of Mr James's pastoral care of his district.

There is a knock on the door.

Mrs Henry: Come in Mr James, it's nice to see you. Just take a seat.
Mr James: Thank you Mrs Henry, and how are you tonight?
Mrs Henry: Well . . . not really very . . .
Mr James: It must be the weather. It has really been very cold recently, and that wind we have been having! I was just saying to the minister, we'll have to be looking again at the heating system.
Mrs Henry: I'm really feeling quite upset.
Mr James: And you've been keeping so well recently. Mrs Brown was saying how you'd been doing so well since you came out of hospital.
Mrs Henry: I know but . . .
Mr James: You had a really tough time when you were in for that operation, but it seems to have made all the difference to your leg.
Mrs Henry: Yes, my leg is fine now and although I've been using a stick I feel I'm getting about much better. But it's not that . . .
Mr James: Well, I'm sure you'll soon be throwing the stick away, and you'll be back dancing again at the next church social.
Mrs Henry: Well, I don't know about that!
Mr James: How's your family? Your husband? Still playing golf on Sunday mornings?
Mrs Henry: Bob's fine! But young Billy's causing me some worry.
Mr James: Fine lad that! I watched him play football the other day and he was the star of the team.

The conversation goes on in the same manner until Mrs Henry goes to make a cup of tea. Over tea, Mr James discusses the minister's sermon, the church's financial position, and then leaves.

Mr James: Goodbye Mrs Henry, and thank you for the cup of tea. It was good to see you looking so well. Remember if you want to talk, just give me a ring.

Now discuss together:

- The issues raised.
- How Mrs Henry and Mr James may be feeling.
- How you would do it differently.

Responding

While we are listening we are also responding.

While we are listening we are also responding to the other person.

We shall not be saying very much because we do not want to interrupt the person who is sharing something with us. We shall be making reassuring gestures and noises to encourage the sharing. Going beyond this can be difficult.

We can be tempted to interrupt the flow of the other person's story by introducing our own story: 'That reminds me of when I was . . .'

Another temptation is to try to show the person that their situation is not as bad as they think:

'You think that's bad. Wait until I tell you about . . .'

Another unhelpful response is to leap in, often remarkably quickly, with: 'I know exactly how you feel.'

We may say this well-meaningly. It is good to recognise that such a statement is untrue. We can never know exactly how anyone else feels about anything. Most of the time we can only think of how *we* might feel in a similar situation. It takes a lot of careful listening and careful responses to get beyond this point.

All of the above responses are in fact blocking devices which impede good communication. Responses like these discount (p. 35) the person. They invite the person to feel discouraged about going on with their story with us

We need to give people space and time when they are sharing a difficulty with us. Attentive silence is a very helpful response when someone needs to find the right word, think through an issue, recall a situation. The gift of an accepting silence communicates:

> I value you enough to wait until you have got the right word, thought the issue through, expressed yourself as you want to.

We need to recognise that because of *our* anxieties we often interrupt, so breaking the silence.

We are anxious because we wonder what to say when the other person stops speaking—how to solve their problem, deal with their difficulty or ease their pain. This will lead us to make very unhelpful and uncaring responses.

In most situations, if not all, it is the other person who is best qualified to deal with their problem, and in fact the only person who can ultimately deal with it.

We may well have good things from our own experience which would be helpful to share, but our primary task as carers is to offer supportive acceptance. We do this in a way which helps the other person to see their problem in a new light, to find new resources and to be able to make their own decisions.

In most situations, if not all, it is the other person who is best qualified to deal with their problem, and in fact the only person who can ultimately deal with it.

When someone is sharing strong feelings it is not helpful to say things like:

'Come on now. Don't feel upset/angry/frightened.'
'There's no need for you to feel like that.'

What a person feels belongs to them. It is important that people feel their feelings. They do not need to be rescued from their feelings. They need their feelings to be listened to and accepted. They need to express their feelings and to work out what they are going to do with them.

Our task is to do the listening and the accepting and then to be supportive as the other person works their feelings through.

Touch can be a very appropriate response when used sensitively, recognising that different people react differently to being touched. In a very real sense, if it is a genuine communication of care, touch says: 'I'm in touch with you.' Touch can often say what words cannot.

Earlier we said that it is important to 'hear' what the other person's body is communicating. Our body language is also important. The other person must be able to 'hear' from our body that we are really listening to them. How we are sitting, our facial expression, our eye contact (without staring the other person out!), are important to our response, sending messages about our interest and wish to hear and understand what is being shared with us. It is soul-destroying to be sharing something difficult and painful with someone who is slouching, with eyes half-closed or glancing at a watch.

Checking out

Through our listening and caring responses we develop our understanding of what the other person is communicating. Words, however, can have different meanings and associations for different people. Feelings can be misinterpreted. We can mistake depression for anger. Our attention can wander or we can miss something as we

Our task is to do the listening and the accepting and then to be supportive as the other person works their feelings through.

think about what we have just heard, or prepare for what we are next to say. *We require to check out that what we have heard is what has been said and meant.*

Reflective listening

A particularly effective way of doing this is by what is known as *reflective listening.* We use ourself as a mirror, reflecting back what has been said to us. We may say things like:

> 'Let me get this straight in my head. You said that . . . and that . . . and so you think . . .'

> 'I understand that you have a strong feeling about what you have told me and that it is causing you pain.'

The other person is being provided with a reflection of what he or she has been communicating and with the opportunity to rectify any error in our understanding. If corrections are made we can reflect back the corrections, checking out that we have now got it right and that the other person has been accurately heard. This encourages the dialogue to continue.

This reflective listening also helps the other person to hear what he or she has said. It can also help the person to get more in touch with their feelings. We might reflect back:

> 'You've used the word "niggled" more than once to describe what you feel about . . . I think I hear something stronger than that.'

The person may reply that the feeling is simply that of feeling niggled or begin to realise that there is more going on inside them that needs to be dealt with. The person might well have known this, of course, but now, because of our response, may feel able to share with us in more depth.

In a situation where a person's words are saying one thing while the language of their body is sending a different message we might say:

> 'I'm glad to hear you say that things are going well for you now, but I get the impression that you are sad about something.'

That response reflects back the two messages which we have heard—the words spoken and the body's apparent sadness. It invites the person to feel understood (or at least that we are trying to understand) and to consider, and perhaps share more of, the sadness. The invitation can, of course, be declined.

Great care must be taken not to impose our own interpretations on a situation. A response like, 'You must feel guilty about that', may invite the person to add another burden, the burden of guilt, to what is already being carried.

Often when someone is sharing a concern with us we have to take in and understand a torrent of words. If we are to understand we may have to step gently in with something like:

> 'Can I stop you there, just for moment, while I check out with you what you have been saying?'

We can then try to summarise the main strands of what has been said, as they appear to us.

Summarising

Summarising is a selective reflecting back of what we believe to have been the main aspects of what has been shared.

Other checking out responses are:

> 'Earlier you said . . . and now you have just said . . . How are these connected?'

> 'Would you say that you are feeling irritated or angry?'

> 'I'm not sure where Mr X fits into the picture. You said he . . . but what is his relation to . . .?'

Sharing our lack of understanding shows that we care enough to get it right; that we are not just some sponge-like kind of listener. It can also help the other person to clarify their own understanding and means of expression.

When we accept a correction about something, even if we do not agree with the correction, we are communicating that we accept the *person* to whom we are listening. *What helps most is the sharing and the thinking-through process of the person who is expressing some concern to us*. We must guard against trying to persuade them of the rightness of our views. *Acceptance of the person, while not necessarily agreeing with what they think, say or do, is what helps a person most of all to decide to change.* We see this clearly in the life of Jesus, in, for example, his relationship with Zacchaeus (Luke 19:1–10).

Reflective listening is a much more caring way of responding than the common response of telling someone what we think they ought to feel, say, think or do.

When using reflective listening expressions like the following are *not* used:

'Don't talk like that!' (*ordering*)
'If you do that you'll be sorry!' (*threatening*)
'Christians should never feel like that!' (*moralising*)
'I suggest you pray about it.' (*advising*)
'When I was your age things like that didn't worry me.' (*lecturing*)
'How can you possibly say that?' (*criticising*)
'Who do you think you are?' (*shaming*)
'That's your need to be needed raising its ugly head again.' (*diagnosing*)
'Everyone has times like these.' (*sympathising*)
'Forget it. Things will work out fine.' (*withdrawing*)

Some of these responses may be appropriate in certain situations, but they are not reflective listening responses.

Reflective listening is a much more caring way of responding than the common response of telling someone what we think they ought to feel, say, think or do.

- It is not judgemental.
- It does not manipulate.
- It checks out its understanding, communicating a genuine concern for the person.
- It enables the other person, if they so wish:
    to learn about him/herself;
    to share at a deeper level;
    to discover their own resources.

Reflective listening requires trust

We need to trust that the other person can handle their feelings and work through their problem. We need also to trust ourselves, because, as we come to understand more fully what the other person is communicating, our own feelings and attitudes may require to change.

Reflective listening is only to be used when:

We really do want to hear and understand what the other person has to say.

- We have the time and the willingness to use it.
- We want to care and are prepared to accept attitudes and feelings which may be very different from our own.

Reflective listening is not to be used if:

- We do not have the time.
- We are not willing to accept what we might hear.
- Our intention is to give our opinions, our wisdom, our solutions.
- We are not prepared to care for the person.
- We are only willing to reflect back words and ideas while ignoring feelings.
- There is, in fact, no problem.
- The other person does not want what they are saying to be reflected back to them.

For thinking through

Practising reflective listening

In the following situations, read what the person has said until you understand:

1 What the speaker is communicating.
2 What the speaker's feelings are.

Write down what you would consider to be a reflective listening response.

Situation 1:

Widower of 80 'I like to sit in the garden here when the weather is fine. I look at the roses and I feel she is here with me, admiring them. She loved these roses—used to fill the house with them at this time of year.'

Situation 2:

Heather (whose nine-year old son was killed in a road accident) 'It has been six weeks now. Everyone else is back to normal. My life will never be the same again. When the children come out of school and down the street here shouting to each other, I can hardly bear to listen.'

Situation 3:

Young father (the day after he has been told that his new baby is severely mentally handicapped) 'They must be trying to cover something up! Joan's healthy and I'm healthy, so how can it possibly "just happen" that we have a child like that? Do you think they could have damaged his brain at the delivery? Did they leave Joan too long in labour? I'm going to get to the bottom of this if it's the last thing I do!'

Share your responses with some fellow-elders. Help one another to decide what would be the most caring responses.

Now try to put reflective listening and checking out into practice in the situations you come across, where there are clearly difficulties in communicating.

Checking out with yourself

It is easy to fall into the trap of thinking that real caring requires a vast amount of experience of all of life's situations and difficulties and that it means being able to give people solutions to their problems. Certainly to be genuinely caring is no lightweight thing. It takes time, energy and skill. But it does not mean having a compendium of good advice, a set of ready answers and solutions, and an armful of life-belts to thrust down and around people's necks!

Caring is first and foremost an attitude. It is a concern for the wellbeing of others. Caring values people. It therefore does not force the carer's thoughts, feelings, beliefs and advice on other people. Rather it tries to enable the cared-for to become more aware of their own value and God-given potential.

In all our *listening* and *responding* and *checking out* it is important to listen to, respond to, and check out *what is going on inside our own self and why we are responding in the way we are.* We can ask ourselves a number of useful questions:

Caring is first and foremost an attitude—a concern for the wellbeing of others.

- Am I trying to rescue the other person when he/she doesn't need it.
- Am I making judgemental statements?
- Am I giving analyses of their behaviour and feelings?
- Am I offering instant solutions?

49

- Am I making these kinds of responses:
  - because I need to feel needed?
  - because I need people to look up to me?
  - because I need to keep people dependent on me?
  - because I need to fulfil other people's expectations?

If the answer to any of these questions is 'yes', then we may have to ask:

- Am I focusing upon the other person or upon myself?

Caring is a way of relating to people which has more to do with the acceptance of people as they are than as we think they ought to be. It is a real focusing on the other person.

The result of this caring is that the person cared for, and often the carer, are helped to grow into fuller, freer, more joyful living— experiencing the enthusiasm we talked about in chapter 1.

While the listening and responding skills we have been talking about require to be practised and developed, the importance of spontaneity should be recognised. There is no *one* right way to care. There are certain constants and we can check ourselves out in the light of them, asking:

- Am I being *genuine*—being myself—with no airs and graces, no false piety, no superiority?
- Am I being *accepting*—of people as they are and not as I want them to be, allowing the other person to be themself?
- Am I showing *respect*—identifying something in the other person which I can respect and about which I can communicate something positive?
- Am I demonstrating *confidentiality*—knowing and letting it be known that what is shared with me is not mine to share with others without the sharer's permission?
- Am I being an *enabler*—recognising that it is the sharer who does the work while the listener enables the sharer to think through their situation and what they are going to do about it.

We recommend (1) placing less emphasis upon *doing for* a person:

- jumping in with solutions *etc*, which even if 'correct', discount the other person and their power to deal with their situation;

and (2) placing more emphasis upon *being with* a person:

- listening and responding to the person;

Caring is a way of relating to people which has more to do with the acceptance of people as they are than as we think they ought to be. It is a real focusing on the other person.

- demonstrating our acceptance of the person;
- inviting them to get in touch with their own power to deal with their situation;
- providing a *listening presence*, which is one of the greatest gifts one person can give to another.

With an emphasis on *being with* we can better resist the part of us which wishes to jump in and *do for*. It also helps us to resist the temptation we may feel to run away for fear of having an inadequate compendium of advice and being short on life-belts! *Besides, being with is God's way of caring and our caring has, surely, to be modelled on God's caring.*

For thinking through

On a sheet of paper draw the following diagram.

1 +	2 —
3 **?**	

Write

1 What you are pleased about in your caring.
2 What you are unhappy about in your caring.
3 How you can strengthen or develop what you have in 1 and how you can work on and change what you have in 2.

Modelling God's care

Empathy

The last response most people want, having shared a painful experience, is sympathy because that can feel patronising. Something deeper is called for. That something has been called *'empathy'*.

It is not easy to describe what this word means. The following quotations give us some idea of the meaning of empathy:

> The power of entering into another's personality and imaginatively experiencing his/her experiences.
>
> *Chambers Twentieth Century Dictionary*

> Empathy is the ability to perceive accurately the feelings of another person and the ability to communicate this understanding to him/her.
>
> E H Kalisch

> More than simple understanding: feeling with and in the client's (other person's) world.
>
> E L La Monica

> Imagine a person who has fallen into a ditch.
>
> The sympathetic helper goes and lies in the ditch with him and bewails the situation with him.
>
> The unsympathetic helper stands on the bank and shouts to the victim, 'Come on, get yourself out of that ditch!'
>
> The empathic helper climbs down to the victim but keeps one foot on the bank, thus being able to help the victim out of the trouble onto firm ground again.
>
> Verena Tschudin

> Without empathy there is no basis for helping.
>
> R R Carkhuff

Empathy is offering our presence to another person—by listening, by communicating that we are listening, and by checking out that what we have heard is what the other person has said.

Empathy is offering our presence to another person—by listening, by communicating that we are listening, and by checking out that what we have heard is what the other person has said.

Empathy is not feeling what *we* would feel in the other person's situation. It is the endeavour to feel what *they* are feeling and experiencing.

Empathy is being with the other person—sitting where they sit, standing in their shoes, walking in their moccasins, feeling where their boot pinches.

The writers of the Bible experienced this presence and closeness of God.

Enoch spent his life in fellowship with God.

Genesis 5:22

Underneath are the everlasting arms.

Deuteronomy 33:27

I will be with you as I was with Moses. I will not leave you or desert you.

Joshua 1:5

Even though I go through the deepest darkness . . . you are with me.

Psalm 23:4

This is precisely what the Christian Gospel proclaims when it talks about the Incarnation—God's coming to *be with* us in the person of Jesus.

Pastoral care is about modelling God's care as we see it in the Bible and particularly in the person of Jesus, and as we, too, can experience it.

If we are to love people, as God does, we must first *listen* to them. We need in a patient and disciplined way to learn to hear what they are actually saying with their words, their silences, their body language. We need to turn the volume down on our own internal chattering.

If we are to love like this we have to respond appropriately—not discounting by telling or avoiding, but by trying to *be with* the person:

- Checking out our understanding.
- Trying to sit where the person sits.
- Encouraging a person to be responsible for their own choices and actions.
- Enabling a person to be in touch with their own resources and the resources in which we all share.
- Providing a listening presence which comforts and strengthens even in life's extremities.

To love like this is to reach out to the whole person with the whole of ourself. It is about developing an open, caring relationship in which

Pastoral care is about modelling God's care as we see it in the Bible and particularly in the person of Jesus, and as we, too, can experience it.

'We know that in all things God works for good *with* those who love him.'
(Romans 8:28)

it is safe to let go of the masks we hide behind, the barriers of separation we erect, and the often destructive roles we play which spoil life in God's 'garden'.

This is the way Jesus related to people, including people who were devalued and discounted by the religion and society of his day (Luke 19:1–9). He listened to people, heard their need and responded in a way which left the responsibility with the other person, while also inviting them to be in touch with a new power.

When we listen to those who share with us when we visit them in their homes; when we listen to their joys and sorrows, we are modelling God's care for his people. We listen and respond in love to enable them to discover more of the fulness of life which is the birthright of all of us.

We enter into a covenant or contract with them—whether or not it is specifically stated—to accept them as they are and to care for them no matter what they do or do not do. Our relationship is not conditional upon their being 'good' members or their being members at all. We shall not reject them even if their suffering is the result of wrong choices they have made. We shall continue to *be with* them, sharing as much of their life as is possible and modelling God's care so that *dialogue* is possible between them and God.

For further reading

People Skills, Robert Bolton.
Still Small Voice, Michael Jacobs, SPCK, 1982.
Swift to Hear: Facilitating Skills in Listening and Responding, Michael Jacobs, SPCK, 1985.
Listening to Others, Joyce Huggett, Hodder Christian Paperbacks, 1988.

For thinking through

Think about situations, relationships and problems which people in your district shared with you the last time you visited them.

Note them down on a piece of paper. Choose one.

Imagine yourself back on that visit.

- How did you respond?
- How did you feel?
- Would you respond differently now?
- If so, what would you say and do?

Repeat this process for the other visits. Destroy the piece of paper.

Choose from the following passages and discuss what they teach about modelling God's care.

- Matthew 19:16–22
- Luke 15:11–32
- Luke 17:11–19
- Luke 19:1–10
- John 8:1–11
- John 11:28–37
- John 21:15–19
- Acts 2:43–47

Share an experience when someone effectively modelled God's care to you.

In what ways do you see yourself modelling God's care to others?

Share with one another—listening to and accepting each other's ways of modelling God's care.

4 Praying with those whom we visit

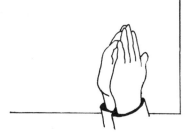

Perhaps in your district you have an elderly and infirm person. Making a cup of tea for that person may not be part of your job description as an elder. It can, however, be an appropriate, caring and much appreciated thing to do. It would not be separate from what had been going on throughout the visit. If it is clearly part of our on-going relationship, it can be, in an almost sacramental way, *a tangible expression of your caring*.

Similarly, praying with people you visit may not be part of your job description but it, too, can be an appropriate, caring and much appreciated thing to do if it arises naturally out of the visit and the on-going relationship.

Prayer needs to be understood as something just as practical and natural as tea-making. It can express in a tangible way that we care and that our caring is part of God's caring. It can add something quite special to our visit—another dimension—and as a result it can help in a way in which nothing else can.

Obviously, just as we need to know how to make a cup of tea before offering to make it for someone else, so prayer needs to be part of our life.

Prayer is like many activities which, once practised, can become second nature to us. Think of what it was like when learning to ride a bike or to swim. In the early stages it felt, for most of us, that we would never learn it. Gradually, however, through listening to our teacher, through learning and practising, how to ride the bike came to us. The know-how became absorbed into our being so that we no longer had to think about and remember the instructions. A new skill became part of us, enriching our life. So it is with prayer.

It also needs to be said about prayer, as about other things, that some people experience more difficulty than other people. A bad teacher or poor learning and practising on our part can lead to difficulties.

For someone with an out-of-date picture of God, one which has not changed from childhood days, praying as an adult may have difficulties. J B Phillips in his book *Your God is Too Small* (Epworth Press) lists the 'unreal gods':

- Resident policeman
- Grand old man
- Meek-and-mild
- Second-hand God
- Parental hangover
- Heavenly bosom
- Managing director
- Pale Galilean

We do well to study what Jesus teaches about God—about whom he says—'He who has seen me has seen the Father' (John 14:9).

Some people are inhibited about praying because they feel unworthy. We need not choose (see p 81) to suffer this inhibition, not if we follow Jesus' teaching. Think of the picture of God offered in his parable of the Prodigal Son in Luke 15. The picture is of a father who sees his son while the boy is a 'great way off ' and runs to meet him; a father who welcomes him back into an open relationship, without any conditions and with no recriminations.

Another common difficulty, especially in leading prayers with other people, is anxiety about using the 'right' words and praying 'properly'. From Jesus we learn that prayer is part of our relationship with God. Have a look at Matthew 6:5–14 and 7:7–11.

If prayer arises out of our relationship with God then it is not special language and structure which count, but rather what lies below the words. Some of the most meaningful prayers can be silent ones—no words, just thoughts and feelings and togetherness.

Prayer is about being open to God who meets us where we are and at whatever stage we are, no matter how far from perfection. It is important to recognise that prayer is not a static activity. It isn't something which has been achieved when the right language has been learned and some particular level of piety attained. It is better to think of it in terms of a journey or a process, in terms of a developing relationship with God. It has to be worked at, as does any relationship of any real value.

We can get help with our praying from the Bible and the writings and experience of other people, but—*prayer is about praying!*

At the end of chapter 2 we talked about praying *for* the people we visit and listening for what God may have to say to us about them. Modelling God's care may also involve us in praying with them. Like the cup of tea mentioned earlier, prayer with those whom we visit is not something to be tagged on, but something which arises naturally out of our relationship with them.

If prayer arises out of our relationship with God then it is not special language and structure which count, but rather what lies below the words. Some of the most meaningful prayers can be silent ones—no words, just thoughts and feelings and togetherness.

'Hour of prayer'

The part that devotions play in a Christian's life will vary from individual to individual. If I am about to describe the content of my own hour of prayer, it is only because each of us can learn from the other.

For my hour of prayer I rise at 6.30 *am*. This to some may seem heroic, but it is nothing of the kind for me. I have reached the stage in life, when we can do with little sleep, and am usually wearily awake at 6 *am* and unable to sleep longer. I have found the early hour delightful. The world is still quiet, and as my study faces east, through my window for much of the year I can watch each new day being marvellously fashioned in broadening light.

Being the creature I am, I work roughly to timetable. The first half-hour I spend in meditation.

For quarter of an hour I read some suitable book. After reading for quarter of an hour, I turn to an extract from *Lord of the Journey*, an anthology of Christian spirituality and think about it for five minutes. Then I turn to my Bible, usually The *Good News Bible*. I used to read the passage prescribed by 'Pray Today,' but by this for months at times I was directed from the gospels, from which I never want to be so long separated. Now I read the 'Pray Today' lectionary with my wife before bedtime, and for my hour of prayer read a short passage from one of the gospels. During my active ministry I used to read a passage from the Bible every morning along with some commentary. In this way I got through all Peake's commentary of the Bible from cover to cover, and many others including all William Barclay's commentaries on the books of the New Testament. I believe that this was good, for there is much a minister ought to know about the Bible. But I confess my Bible reading then was too often distracted by searching for texts from which to preach to others. Now retired, free from this distraction, and putting all my commentaries aside, I find much more profit and enjoyment in simply listening to what the gospel passage has to say to me personally. I read each passage very slowly then think about it for about ten minutes, and I have been repeatedly astonished how aptly the Word begins to speak when listened to.

I have found truths and aspects of the truth quite new to me to start alive from even the most familiar passages.

The next half-hour I spend in prayer. To lead me to the point of contemplative prayer I sometimes use the guidance provided in 'Kyrie Eleison': sometimes use the sequence of prayers followed in church worship—adoration, confession, petition and thanksgiving. Sometimes I make deliberate use of the Lord's Prayer. Then in contemplation I try to enter that wordless communion with God, in which we come to Him and His love. If I have not already made use of the Lord's Prayer, I usually close this quarter of an hour by slowly reciting it.

The remaining quarter of an hour I use for intercession. I find that as we are awakened to the love of God, our growing love for others will want to give a larger place for intercession. First I pray for the church, and especially for revival for our own Church of Scotland, in view of the reports made on our Life Style by our Board of Social Responsibility. Then I use the scheme for intercession in 'Pray Today'. As an associate of the Iona Community I next pray for the listed members and fellow associates for each day. I close by remembering my own acquaintances who are in special need, and lastly the members of my own family.

There can be no general prescription for the time we allow to our devotions. Much will depend on individual temperament. 'Don't linger about the Audience chamber', was D L Moody's advice which will certainly appeal to many. The Mary-Martha tension is always with us. We mustn't make a fetish of filling up a prescribed time, thinking that the longer we are at our prayers, the holier we will necessarily become. We should be guided by what we ourselves find most happy. If we prolong our prayers into boring ourselves, have pity on God. At times our necessary business will affect the time we are free to spend. The most sensible advice I know to the point was given by Dr Rainy to his son, when the young man was passing through a time of especial business: 'It cannot be easy for you to maintain your devotions at this time, I suggest that if you have only five minutes for Bible reading, you spend two on reading and three for thinking about it in God's presence. The same with your prayers. Shorter prayers if you must, but think a little before you begin.' Five minutes heart-to-heart communion with God will be of more use than one whole hour spent in vague or wandering thoughts of God. On the other hand the more we come to know the love of God, the more time we will want to spend with Him.

This article, written by the Rev Dr George Reid, appeared in the August 1987 edition of Life and Work *and is reprinted with kind permission.*

To be open to the God whose living presence is around and within us, is to be open to the same God who is present in those whom we are visiting. This moves the focus from *the act of saying a prayer* to *the relationship we have with the people*.

About this relationship Jesus says:

> Where two or three come together in my name, I am there with them.
>
> Matthew 18:20

He is present in the room and in the relationship. An act of prayer recognises this and offers the relationship to God. What we need to guard against is making prayer some kind of activity separate from our human relationship.

A key word with regard to prayer is *openness*. A prayer comes out of openness to our inner self, to the inner selves of other people, and to God. Part of our openness to another person is the reflecting back to them of what they have communicated. Prayer *with* the people we are visiting is the reflecting back of the whole of our pastoral visit within the context of our on-going relationship with them. The 'raw materials' of our prayer will be the topics of conversation and the people involved—their feelings, joys, problems, and the warmth of the relationship.

In pastoral prayer we are enabling all those in the room to gather their thoughts and feelings in the presence of God.

Prayer does not conform to rules. It is the attitude or atmosphere of our lives. It is a way of life. Each one of us prays differently because each of us is different from all others. Each one of us is unique. What unites us in our praying is our openness, our need and our belief that prayer works. All christians pray 'in the name of Jesus' because he is our authority.

Here are some guidelines which will help you in your pastoral prayers:

Guidelines

1   Prayers need to be *part of your life* before you begin to lead the prayers of others. Part of our embarrassment and unease about praying in the home we visit is that we do not practise it

'Where two or three come together in my name, I am there with them.'
(Matthew 18:20)

ourselves, or that we practise it infrequently. Our embarrassment may also be due to a lack of practice in praying with other people.

2 Read and absorb the *prayers of others* and what they have said about prayer. Read what the *Bible* says about prayer—especially the prayers of the psalmists and Jesus.

3 Prayer ought to be truly part of the visit, not just tagged on at the end. It must *never become a ritual*—something which is done, no matter what else is missed out. Rather, if you pray do so sensitively and appropriately.

4 *Don't trap people* into agreeing to you saying a prayer. Many people will find it difficult to say 'No, thank you', while inwardly wishing to do so. This can have a detrimental effect on your visit and on subsequent visits. Prayer ought not to be felt as a threat because it has been imposed even for the best reasons. Feeling that you want to pray is not necessarily a good enough reason for praying on a pastoral visit.

5 Remember you are *leading the prayers of others* when you are praying, you therefore need to take into consideration how they feel and what their needs are.

6 In some circumstances it may be more appropriate for you to *pray later*. It may even be more effective if those whom you are visiting are uncomfortable with, or opposed to you praying in their home.

7 Be careful with such phrases as *'I'll remember you in my prayers!'* or *I'll pray for you'*. Even if you do not mean the words to be patronising or judgemental they can often sound that way. They may be heard by those to whom you are speaking as indicating that you think that they are in need of correction and that, almost behind their backs, you will enlist divine aid.

8 Beware *ulterior motives* in your praying—such as the need to have a 'holy bit' at the end of the visit. Prayer can also be used as a way of ending a visit when other methods have failed to provide a space big enough for you to get out of your armchair, onto your feet and moving in the general direction of the door. Perhaps, most of all, prayer can be used as a way of getting at people via God, in a form which they are unlikely to interrupt.

SESSION MATTERS

In at the deep end

Should an elder pray when he visits a house in his district?

If beneath this question there lies the question of whether an elder should ever pray in the homes of his/her district I would believe the answer is a clear affirmative. Christians should be able to pray together. It would be hard to disagree with that, so why should those who have been ordained as the spiritual leaders of a congregation not be permitted to pray with their fellow-members in their districts? Indeed they should be willing and able so to do.

I don't think we should, however, make a law out of a means of Grace. There may be times when it is not appropriate to lead a prayer on a visit. Faced by a non-member husband, who resents his wife's involvement in the congregation, might not be the time. On the other hand, it might be just the time. My experience tells me that there are far more people who welcome being led in prayer than I, at one time, would have believed. We must remember, however, that this is not something we, to satisfy our needs and self-expectations, do to others regardless of their needs and wishes.

If we haven't done this before what's the best way to start?

Perhaps in your district you have a housebound member who is no longer able to take his/her place in the pews, no longer able to hear the Scriptures read at a service of Worship. Remind the person that he is still very much part of God's family. Ask if he would like you to read a passage of Scripture with him—perhaps the 23rd Psalm. Few will decline the invitation. After the reading—quietly, simply and sincerely—lead a prayer thanking God for the faith offered to us in that psalm: for our belonging to the Church, and for His blessing on your fellow-member and yourself.

You may find that, following this, your visit begins. If, however, you leave at that point you will have made a pastoral visit, having pointed your fellow-Christian to his or her God.

Perhaps a new family has come into your district. Before you leave on your first visit you could suggest that together you ask for God's blessing on their new home. You might read Jesus' teaching at the end of the Sermon on the Mount about building a house on rock rather than on sand. Ask for God's blessing on this new home, giving thanks for the privilege you have of being part of it and seeking God's help to ensure that its foundations are firmly based.

I don't know what the 'best way to begin' is. I do know that if we are to learn to swim we must get into the water—and we must get more than our toes wet.

For further reading

The Plain Man's Book of Prayers, William Barclay, Fontana, 1959.
More Prayers for the Plain Man, William Barclay, Fontana, 1962.
Epilogues and Prayers, William Barclay, Student Christian Movement, 1963.
Prayers of Life, Michel Quoist, Logos Books, 1963.
You: Prayer for Beginners and Those Who have Forgotten How, Mark Link, Argus, 1976.

For thinking through

Share your experiences of praying with people in your district.

Thinking back to these experiences, do any of the guidelines on pp 58f seem particularly relevant?

Are there other guidelines you could pass on from your experience?

The following passages from the Bible may be found helpful when visiting people in need of pastoral care:

- Lamentations 3 (19–27, 31, 32)
- Psalms 23, 51 (1–12), 103 (8–14), 121, 130, 139
- Matthew 5 (3–10), 6 (25–34)
- John 14 (17)
- 1 Peter 4 (12–16)

Add to the list passages you know which are helpful.

Write short prayers which you could use in different pastoral situations, *eg* bereavement, illness, time of celebration, threatened redundancy, new home, *etc*.

It would be of value if, in small groups, your fellow-elders could share in the doing of these things and combined experiences gathered together for all to share.

5 Situations we face as elders

In pastoral work of the eldership it is important to recognise that we are *caring for people* rather than *dealing with problems*. Focusing on the people, rather than the difficult situations, means that our caring helps people to tackle their own situations, encouraged by our presence, understanding and support. This also means that we can be less anxious about the situations and concentrate our energies on caring for the people.

Nevertheless, people are not met in a vacuum. We meet them in their homes, in the context of their family life and in the midst of their everyday experiences. Part of our caring is to listen to the context of their life—the situations they find themselves in at the time of our visit.

In this chapter we look at a number of common situations and offer pointers to some important things to listen for. They are not rules, but rather clues or guidelines to help you listen and respond.

We would encourage you to make use of the various resources available to you—books, video cassettes, training courses—to help you handle stressful situations. A number have been listed.

We would remind you of all that we said in chapter 3 about listening and responding in a caring way, accepting the reality of the other person's situation and trying to be present with them in *their* situation.

Visiting the ill   ► ► ►

To visit your members when they are ill, in hospital or at home, can be a powerful expression of your care for them.

It can be very helpful when news, especially during hospital visiting hours is in scarce supply, because of restrictions suffered by the patient and by the relatives whose lives revolve around to-ing and fro-ing from the hospital. The elder can help to oil the wheels of conversation, but remember what we said in chapter 2 about the

Illness

The Minister speaks to you at the end of the service and says 'Mrs Hopkins has gone into hospital—I hear she is very ill. I know her husband and young daughter will be at their wits end. Will you go and see what you can do?'

What do you do? What is there to

say? When do you go? What about the family—do you visit them too? Will they not feel this is an intrusion? How will you cope?

different levels of communication.

Personal experience has taught us that a visit paid during visiting hours can be difficult, requiring more sensitivity than is sometimes given to it. It can for example be a great intrusion on the needs of the patient and his or her family. This is true when the patient does not have the energy—physical, mental or emotional—to concentrate on visitors other than members of the family, especially if the conversation is on a banal or cliché level. The relatives may also resent such talk and find it an intrusion on their time with their loved one. All that patient and family may need is to rest in the possibly wordless, hand-holding comfort of their togetherness.

Ministers, fortunately, can, with permission, call at times other than the official visiting hours. Sometimes arrangements can be made for other people, *eg* elders, to do the same. Care, however, must be taken in hospitals which permit long visiting hours. Patients can, whether at home or in hospital, become worn out by a continuous stream of visitors! Since people feel differently about this, it is important to listen, check out what you hear and see, and respond appropriately.

Some pointers

- In the case of serious illness, members of the family can be put under a lot of stress because of constant phone calls enquiring about the health of the patient. You may have to work hard at keeping up-to-date without adding to this burden. If the family return home from hospital at 8.45 pm and the phone is still ringing at 11.45 pm, this is extremely tiring on top of the emotional strain of the visit itself. However it is done, permission should be sought from the patient's family for the elder to visit. It is also important to know whether this visit would be welcomed or not, and when it would be appropriate for you to call. It is important to express concern but without imposing oneself.
- At some stages, and with people who are very close to the family, both patient and family can find communication difficult. They do not have the energy for cliché talk, nor do they feel able to go beyond the control stage of emotion which we refer to on p.31f.

This may mean that your visits may have to be brief. Because you are close to the person concerned it may be difficult for the patient to allow him or herself to unburden to you in a time of heavy emotional crisis. Take this as a compliment.

- Remember those who have to watch and wait. It is so easy to direct most of your attention on to the patient. 'How is he today?' etc., and to forget the needs of those who have to anxiously watch and wait as they see a loved one struggling to survive and who themselves have to return home to a lonely house with their anxiety.

- Remember the very positive ministry of letter writing and card sending. It can mean so much in the loneliness of illness to know that people are thinking about you. Letters of appreciation can be a great treasure, as can the awareness that people are sharing their concern about the patient with a God who is known not to want his people to be ill. You can also encourage other members of the congregation and friends of the family to write. Don't forget a letter or a card to the members of the family themselves. Visits and letters to them to express your understanding of their difficult situation are just as important and caring.

- Remember how important practical help can be—the offer of help to get in the weekly shopping and, of course, the offer of lifts to and from the hospital. Not everyone has a car at their disposal and buses can be awkward and taxis expensive.

- Remember too, where and when appropriate, what we said in chapter 4 about not just praying *for* but praying *with* the person and his or her family. To help clear the way for this level of ministry you might care to read again what we said about blocks to communication in chapter 2, pp. 32ff.

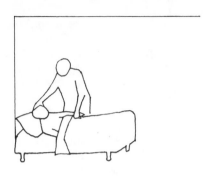

Christian healing

Doctors and nurses work constantly for the comfort and the healing of the sick. Alongside this, a ministry of healing, through prayer and the laying on of hands, offers a specific contribution which does not normally fall within the sphere of the caring professions.

The ministry of prayer may itself open the way for God to heal.

The ministry of the laying on of hands and/or anointing with oil may also be a means of healing. This may take the form of a simple ministry of touch, holding the hand or soothing the brow of the sick person. It may be something which is shared with other elders and church members and involve a simple service of healing.

Such a ministry should not be seen as odd or unusual, but simply as part of the normal life of the Church, the 'Body of Christ', in this world as Christians seek—in a spirit of acceptance, trust and expectation—to find the best that God would have us know and experience as His people.

Frontline Code C 17
'Ministering to the Sick' by Dr Isobel Grigor

For further reading

Health and Healing, Frontline Target Pack, Church of Scotland Department of Education, 1988.

Healing, Francis MacNutt, Bantam Books, 1974.

Prayers for Help and Healing, William Barclay, Collins Fount, 1968.

Visiting the Sick: A Guide for Laity, Norman Hutton, Mowbrays, 1980.

Going into Hospital, David Murray Main, United Reformed Church, 1988.

In Hospital, David Murray Main, United Reformed Church, 1985.

Terminal illness

There are five stages through which a person who has been told they are dying, may pass (Elisabeth Kubler-Ross: *On Death and Dying*):

1 *Denial* of the terminal nature of the illness or even denial of the illness. This may take the form of a belief that the doctor is mistaken.
2 *Anger* at the situation they are in. This may be directed at doctors, family or God.
3 *Bargaining* for more time: 'If only I get a longer time, I promise I shall . . .'
4 *Depression* as the truth sinks in that there is nothing else which can be done. There can be depression over the losing of strength, mobility, bodily functions, ordinary interests and even the impending loss of all that is dear. Fear, worry and helplessness can be overwhelming.
5 *Acceptance* is the positive attitude to what has previously caused anger and despair. The terminally ill person accepts the inevitable and decides to make the best use of the time which is left.

It is helpful to keep these stages in mind when caring for someone who is terminally ill while recognising that, as with bereavement, no two people are the same. Everyone reacts differently and at their own pace and many do not go through all the above stages.

It is also important to keep in mind that people who are diagnosed as being terminally ill may experience 'remission' when the progress of the illness is halted. Recovery may also take place against all the medical odds.

Some helpful ways in which an elder may respond

- *Accept* the terminally ill person at whatever stage they are.
- *Hear* what their feelings are. Recognise the feelings, reflect them back gently and be ready to let the person concerned express and talk about their feelings. It is more destructive to bottle up the feelings than to express them.
- *Reassure* the person concerned that it is alright to have whatever feelings they have and that you will not reject or criticise them.

Terminal illness

Mrs Robertson, an elder, has regularly visited Mr Carter who has been ill for some time.

On this occasion, however, Mrs Robertson is somewhat taken aback when Mr Carter, ill as he is, launches into an attack on the church, the elders and God.

After a very uncomfortable visit, during which she wondered what she had said or done to provoke this, Mrs Robertson reflected on the situation.

Mr Carter has always seemed a gentle man who accepted his illness with a degree of cheerfulness. However, on her last visit a month ago, he had been a little pre-occupied and seemed to be saying that his illness was not as serious as everyone thought and that he would soon be up and about and at church again.

Later in the week it all began to make some sense. Mrs Robertson met Mrs Carter who told her that two days before she had visited them the previous month, Mr Carter had been told that he had terminal cancer.

- *Appropriate touch can be very important.* It communicates that a person is not alone. It is something positive you can do as a response to what you have heard and despite helpless feelings to do anything.
- *Recognise that relatives of the terminally ill and those who care for the dying may pass through similar stages.* They may also become exhausted in their caring, particularly if the dying person's illness is lengthy. It will be part of the elder's caring to recognise the carer's need for support and relief. You may consider suggesting to the carer concerned that you contact some members of the congregation who would be willing to offer to sit with the dying person to enable the carers to have some time to themselves.
- *Be aware that doctors differ about whether or not to tell a patient or the relatives about a terminal illness.* They may not have a general rule but judge each case on its own merits. At an already painful time, tensions can arise when some, or all, of the relatives know that the person is dying. The same is true when the patient knows and the family does not or when all know but keep it secret from each other. It is not possible to say what should be done in all situations.

  We need to be sensitive, to listen and to respond in the way which is most caring for all. This may mean helping relatives to think through what they want to do. It may also mean hearing the 'secret' from the dying person.
- *Be ready to:*

  Share your faith appropriately.
  Take your cue from those you are visiting.
  Recognise your own feelings.

For further reading

On Death and Dying, Elisabeth Kubler-Ross, Tavistock Publications, 1973.
Letting Go: Caring For Dying and Bereaved, Peter Speek and Ian Ainsworth-Smith, SPCK, 1982.

Bereavement ➤ ➤ ➤

There is something wrong with us if we do not feel helpless in the face of another person's grief. The truth is that we *are* helpless. There is nothing that we can say or do which will take the pain away.

Our very presence may be a reminder to the grieving people of God's presence and of the fellowship of the Church to which they perhaps belong—whether or not God or the Church is mentioned.

There are four identifiable stages through which a grieving person moves:

1 *Shock*: Feelings too painful to face are cut off. Mrs Smith is clearly in this stage. The ability to make decisions, plan and organise is impaired. Someone is needed to support and make decisions but without taking over.

2 *Control*: Feelings are controlled for the sake of other people. Many in our culture believe the bereaved ought to be strong and brave.

3 *Regression*: A lot of energy has been used up in holding oneself together and keeping strong feelings in place. The bereaved may become self-centred and introverted, and swamped by bad feelings from the past and fears for the future.

4 *Adaptation*: Bereaved people learn to adapt to the changed situation. They begin to re-own the part of themselves which had been 'invested' in the relationship with the person who died; and start to re-invest in other relationships both existing and new.

It helps to be aware of what is going on in the grieving person and of what stage they are at. Movement from one stage to another is a crucial time for support and encouragement.

The movement from one stage to another does not necessarily flow neatly—but may fluctuate. The bereaved person may be in one stage with one person and in another with someone else. Even with the same person the bereaved person may be at different stages from time to time.

Here are some helpful pointers in caring for the bereaved:

• *Be available*. Be *with* them rather than do *for* them. Give them your telephone number, invite them to call, and to get in touch
• with you if they so wish.
Respond to feelings. Accept how they feel, help them to express

Bereavement

The elder is sitting in the living room of Mrs Smith, whose husband died earlier in the day.

Mr and Mrs Smith had been married for over 40 years and were a devoted couple, whose life had never been easy.

Mrs Smith has two sons and two daughters who, with their respective wives and husbands and children, have recently arrived.

A neighbour has also dropped in for a few minutes.

The elder is anxious, knowing that it is his duty to be there, but cannot think of anything helpful to say. The more he thinks about it the more trite his thoughts become.

What really confuses him is that Mrs Smith does not seem to have grasped what has happened.

Now and again someone breaks down in tears.

their feelings and be ready to share your own feelings. Feelings of guilt and anger are often present alongside feelings of sorrow and despair. It may be helpful to give reassurance that it is alright to have these feelings and to express them—even to God.

- *Encourage talking about the loss* and about the person who has died. If it is possible, share some of your own good memories of the person.
- *Touch* can communicate much when words fail. A touch of the hand, an arm on the shoulder, if not imposed on a resistant person, can be comforting.
- *Offer practical help* when that is possible.
- *Share your faith appropriately*, without preaching or pushing. Know what you believe about life after death and be ready to share your faith gently. When questions like 'Why did this happen to me?' or 'What have I done to deserve this?' are asked in the regression stage, hear them as expressions of pain rather than as questions seeking intellectual answers. Respond to the feelings. Answers can be discussed at a later stage.
- *Pray* when that feels appropriate and keep in mind what we said in chapter 4 about praying *with* people. It can be helpful to be prepared to read an appropriate piece of Scripture.
- *Take your cue* from those whom you are visiting. Different people respond differently to bereavement. Accept them where they are. That acceptance will invite them to move on when they feel ready.
- *Recognise your own feelings*. The grief of others may connect with your feelings about a past loss which you have experienced. If that becomes painful, talk to someone who will listen and accept your feelings and help you to work through your feelings.

For further reading

The Grief Process, Yorick Spiegel, Student Christian Movement, 1977.

Jean's Way, Derek Humphrey, Fontana.

Loss: an Invitation To Grow, Jean C Grigor, Arthur James, 1986.

A Letter of Consolation, Henri Nouwen, Gill and MacMillan, 1983.

The Bereaved Parent, Harriett Schiff, Souvenir Press, 1977.

All in the End is Harvest, Agnes Whitaker, Darton, Longman and Todd/Cruse, 1984.

For thinking through

Individually:

Work out what you believe about life after death

1 What beliefs about life after death do you hold?
2 What beliefs are you not sure about?

In working on these questions consider the following Bible passages, possibly using different translations:

- Psalms

16:1-2, 5-11	22:1-11
23	31:9-14
46	90:1-6
103:8-18	139

- Gospels
  John 11: 17-27; 14:1-7
  Accounts of the Resurrection appearance of Jesus
  Matthew 28
  Mark 16
  Luke 24
  John 20 and 21

- Revelation 21:1-5

What do these passages say to you? Do they help you?

Together

1 In what circumstances would you share what you believe about life after death?
2 What would help you to know when it was appropriate to share your beliefs with a grieving person?
3 What other beliefs about life after death do you come across in your district? What can you learn from these beliefs for your own benefit, and to help you understand those who hold them?

Individually

Meet with someone who experienced a bereavement a few years ago or, if more recently, someone well known to you. Discuss with them what was helpful and unhelpful about the responses from other people to their grief.

Together

Share what you have learned from your research. Make two lists—one of helpful and another of unhelpful responses to grief.

For thinking through

Make a list of experiences of loss which you have had.

Can you recognise stages in the grief process which you went through?

Share your experience and how it may help you in your pastoral work.

Think of the homes in your district.

What losses have people expressed in the time you have known them?

Do any of them have an experience or loss which they have not yet worked through?

How can you help them?

Bereavement and loss of health are not the only *loss experiences* common in life. The four stages of grief mentioned on p. 68:—shock, control, regression adaptation—can apply also to

- *Loss of:*
  Employment
  Faith
  Respect
  Privacy
  Hair
  Friends
  Possessions
  Money
  Senses

- *Loss due to:*
  Going into hospital
  Surgery
  Moving home
  Changing job
  Children going to school
  Children leaving home
  Burglary
  Senility
  Fire

We believe that perhaps every painful experience may have involved in it an experience of loss.

For further reading

Depression

Coping with Crises, Ruth Fowkes, Hodder and Stoughton.

Stress

The Relaxation Response, Albert Benson, Fountain Books, 1975.
Living with Stress, Consumers Association, 1968.

Marriage

Make or Break, Jack Dominian, SPCK, 1984.
I Count: You Count, George Calder, Argus, 1976.

Midlife

Middle Age, M. Fiske, Harper and Row, 1979.

Video cassette

'Pastoral Care', produced jointly by Church of Scotland, United Reformed Church, Presbyterian Church of Wales, Presbyterian Church in Ireland, 1987.

Hidden agendas

Notice the *expected* and *unexpected* elements in that elder's visit.

Expected: The elder knew the family well. She therefore had certain expectations of the visit before she knocked on the door. The conversation started as expected. Everything seemed normal.

Unexpected:

1 It became obvious that something was affecting the conversation: The elder did not know what it was but she was aware of the undercurrent.
2 The father suddenly hit the elder with his angry words about the church, God and the suffering world. It was a bolt from the blue!
3 The father's worry about his daughter's illness was hidden underneath the other levels of the conversation. It had not been brought to the surface but, nevertheless, it had affected the whole course of the visit.

We are aware of what an agenda is with regard to our Session meetings. We may be less aware that there is an agenda for every visit we make. Whether well thought out or not there will be what we want to say and how we want the visit to go. The people we visit will have their agenda—what they expect and want out of our visits.

There can also be *hidden agendas* by which we mean the thoughts, attitudes and especially the feelings which are under the surface and undeclared. They affect the relationship and the conversation without being available for understanding or discussion.

Some pointers

- We could get into all sorts of difficulty by telling the father that he should not question God or by giving him a reasoned explanation for the suffering in the world.
- The father needs someone who will listen to what he is saying and also to what he is not saying. Give him the space and time to surface his hidden feelings and accept him as he expresses his feelings. Invite the surfacing of the hidden.
- Recognise that it is only when the hidden agenda is acknowledged that it can be dealt with. The question 'Why does God . . . .?' often is not seeking an intellectual answer. It

Hidden agendas

The elder calls at the home of a family, well-known to her, and active members of the congregation. She is unaware that the 17-year-old daughter has just been diagnosed as suffering from an illness which will impair the quality of her life and to which there is no known cure.

The conversation goes on normally for some time but it becomes more and more obvious to her that something is wrong.

Eventually the father, who has been unusually quiet, says angrily—'I don't know how you can talk about the church . . . . All this talk about caring for others. We've worked for the church all our lives. Our daughter is a Sunday school teacher. But where does that get us? Why does this so-called loving God allow all this suffering in the world? Just answer me that!'

The elder reels under this onslaught.

Before reading on, take a few minutes to write down what you think you would have said in response. Continue the dialogue, then read what you have written and see what it teaches you.

is a cry of pain regarding something which lies below the question. When it does demand an answer, we can only tell it the way it is for us, and not expect everyone to agree with us.

- It may provide the clue that there is something which needs to be surfaced.

Roles and games

There are three common roles that people play.

1 *Victim:* when we claim to be helpless, incapable and so excused from taking the steps necessary to resolve some difficulty; excused from the effort required to get well, pass an exam or whatever.
2 *Rescuer:* when we, in the guise of being helpful, provide solutions and answers and so keep other people dependent upon us. We may say 'I was only trying to help', but our need to 'ride to the rescue' is far more important to us than the *actual* need of the other person.
3 *Persecutor:* when we ignore, criticise, discount, blame and put down other people believing that we are right, excluding the possibility that the other person could be right or has even the right to be heard.

Victims feel so bad about themselves that they look for *rescuers* or *persecutors*. They feel justified then in feeling bad because they are being persecuted or because not even a rescuer can rescue them.

Rescuers look for victims needing (they think) to be rescued.

Persecutors look for victims to exercise their need to persecute.

Of course there are times when people *are* in a very helpless situation and genuinely need rescuing. A drowning man needs swift rescuing. But what was going on in the scene with the elder was the conscious or unconscious playing of a role. The lady was a *victim* who was inviting the elder to be a *rescuer*. After all he was her elder! But no matter how many solutions he came up with she would have the last words. 'Yes, but . . .' It is likely that she will play a 'Yes, but' game with anyone who is willing to play *rescuer*.

We do not help such a person by our efforts to rescue them. Had the elder listened better, with his eyes as well as his ears, he might have spotted the role being played and avoided the invitation to play

---

Roles and games ◀ ◀

The elder is visiting a lady who has a particular problem. She asks for help and the elder suggests something which might help.

'Yes', the lady says, 'that could be an answer. But you see . . .' She has appreciated the suggestion apparently, but clearly it isn't quite the right answer. The elder tries again.

'Yes', she says, 'I'll think about that but you see . . .'

The elder tries again. After all he is her elder. She is supposed to be able to turn to him for assistance.

This time she smiles and nods her head. The elder inwardly sighs a sigh of relief. 'Yes', she says 'but . . .'

Now the elder begins to feel most uncomfortable. He rides to the rescue with a fourth suggestion as to how the problem might be eased. 'Perhaps you could . . .'

'Yes', she says, 'but . . .'

Some time later the woman gets quite angry and says 'Well I thought I would have at least got some help from an elder!'

The elder wonders what on earth has happened and what he has done wrong.

D

his role. In such a situation we can try, gently but firmly to confront the person with Jesus' question in John 5:6—perhaps by reflecting back (see pp. 45f) what they are playing—and begin to help the person to find their own resources and solution.

At the end of the scene you will have noticed a switch of roles. The victim becomes a *persecutor* and the *rescuer* has become the *victim*. Such a switch is a sure clue to the fact that we are involved in a 'game', not a happy game, a psychological game, in which feelings get hurt.

Non-attenders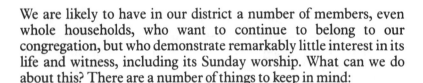

We are likely to have in our district a number of members, even whole households, who want to continue to belong to our congregation, but who demonstrate remarkably little interest in its life and witness, including its Sunday worship. What can we do about this? There are a number of things to keep in mind:

1 *Contract*: Many of our members took their vows a long time ago. They may have been pressured into 'joining the Church' (*eg* by parents prior to marriage). Their contract with God and his Church may have been ill prepared for in poorly led First Communicant's classes. The Session which admitted them may have played down the commitment. Some of our 'members' may be in fact no different from those who do not belong to the Church because they do not have the faith to belong.

2 *Life blows*: Some of our members may have experienced a good First Communicant's class in which faith, enthusiasm and commitment were fostered and demonstrated. Life may have dealt them some heavy blows subsequently. They may not wish to leave the Church but do not see its relevance in the face of these blows. A poverty-stricken congregational lifestyle may be of little interest and help to them.

3 *Little sense of belonging*: Non-attendance on the part of some of our members may be the result of their feeling that they do not belong to the congregation. To become relatively involved people need to know that they are cared for, that they matter. Their talents and skills must be recognised. They need to know that they have a real part to play in the life of the congregation.

Non-attenders

The elder is visiting a husband and wife who are members of the congregation. They have a young family whom they send to Sunday School. The parents now and again attend on a Communion Sunday. Other than that they have little involvement.

They do not wish to give up their membership and sometimes promise to 'do better'. Their promises are never kept.

For thinking through

Individually

- Think of the families in your district who do not go to church.
- Try to think your way into their situation and imagine what their real reasons may be.
- What do you think they are feeling about the church?
- How best can you communicate your acceptance of them and, at the same time, deal with your own frustration?

Together

- Share your own thoughts and listen to those of your fellow elders.
- Encourage and support one another in the plans you have made for dealing with the situations which you have shared.

Some pointers

- *Beware being the heavy parent*: A temptation is to assume the 'persecutor' role, to be like the school attendance officer or the disciplining parent emphasising the 'oughts' and 'shoulds', stressing the vows, once taken and as yet not rescinded. This approach may work (if that's the right word) with a few 'obedient' people, but most adults have had enough of that kind of approach a long time ago and are not likely to respond well to it. Any who do appear to respond may not do so for long, if at all. Their promise to change their ways may simply be their attempt to get the authority figure (in this case, the elder) off their backs, at least for the moment. We all know the child's promise 'I'll never do that again, Dad' which rarely lasts for 24 hours!
- *Beware avoiding the issue*: Another temptation is to seek to avoid the issue by keeping discussion with non-attenders at a cliché or superficial level (p 30). If we do this we do not help the people to take the faith and the Church seriously. Our avoidance may re-inforce their negative attitudes, seeming to indicate that non-participation is not worth discussing. Our avoidance of the issue will certainly not encourage them to believe that *their* involvement matters to us.
- *Recognise conflicting loyalties*: Acceptance of the standards of the non-attenders does not help them to take faith and the Church seriously. We must also consider the discouragement they provide, plus the over-burdening they may cause, to the other members of the congregation. The life of the congregation may be greatly weakened. There is also the very serious obstacle the non-attenders present to those outside the Church. It is not easy to persuade someone to become interested in Christ and his Church when he sees someone who is a 'member' showing no sign of interest in the Church and its activities.

Although as elders we may feel very hesitant about 'discipline', as it has been called, we cannot avoid the issue of the removal from the congregational roll of those who show no evidence of real interest in the Church's work and worship. We shall first do all we can to get alongside such people, seeking to get beyond the excuses and the criticisms to the real reasons for non-participation. We may have to make changes in the lifestyle of the congregation if the real reasons have more to do with us than with the non-attenders. If this is not the case, non-attenders may have to be placed on the roll of lapsed members, with whom a pastoral link is still to be maintained.

For further reading

The following books deal with *Transactional Analysis*, which many Christians find a useful tool in understanding ourselves and our relationships.

A Tool for Christians (Books I (1981) and II (1983)), Jean C Grigor, Church of Scotland Department of Education.
Born to Win, Muriel James and Dorothy Jongeward, Signet, 1971.
I'm OK, You're OK, Thomas Harris, Pan, 1967.
Finding Hidden Treasure, Laura Geiger, Jalmar, 1979.

Asking for money

Asking for money is seldom easy and, understandably, many elders feel uncomfortable about asking for money. It is useful to keep the following in mind.

1 The Church is *not* 'always asking for money'. What is asked of its members is *response* to the love of God and *commitment* to being his Church, to being part of the shared ministry we talked about in chapter 1.
2 Part of our Christian response and commitment is to the work and witness of the local congregation to which we belong as part of the worldwide church. Obviously, local congregations require money to exist as does every other human organisation, including the household registering the protest!
3 The Church's main source of income is the money given by its members. The largest part of the money raised by most congregations is spent on maintaining their own life and witness—*ie*, staff, property, running costs, *etc.* Congregations also contribute towards the wider work of the denomination to which they belong.

Asking for money

The elders are visiting their districts as part of an appeal to the congregation to increase the offerings.

Many of the elders experience, in one way or another, the response 'Not again! The Church is always asking for money!'

When we feel uncomfortable about asking for money, it may help to remember that the church needs people who will offer an opportunity to their fellow members to make their financial response. This is part of our, and their, worship—an expression of what our faith is worth to us. It is an expression of what God means to us.

Some pointers

- Do not get *hooked by criticism*. Do your homework beforehand and know what the financial needs of the Church and congregation are. Be ready to give information about what the money will be used for. Know how much it costs to run your church.
- *Be straight* in your response. Help people to understand the situation and that our financial response is part of our total response to God.
- *Listen* to any complaints and to the feelings, hurts and misunderstanding under them. Respond without criticising and without necessarily agreeing. You will thus be sensitive to the person concerned. Listening helps you to feel less anxious and the person you are visiting to feel accepted.
- Do not take the *criticism personally*. It may feel as if the feelings are aimed at you. However, you are at the receiving end because you are there. Continue to listen to the feelings. You may be helping hurting people more than you think. A visit by a caring person may begin with money and end in healing through listening and acceptance.
- Be careful not to *deny an opportunity* to give because the person concerned may have little money. Many who have little, wish to give what they can. We should not deny them that opportunity. Nevertheless some may not be able to give. The criticisms about asking for money may be covering up their embarrassment.

For thinking through

Can you recognise homes in your district where there are people playing one of the three roles: *persecutor, victim, rescuer*?

- Which role do they invite you to play?
- Do you play the invited role?
- If you do, how could you avoid doing so in the future?

In your district, or wherever, do you *invite* people to play a role with you?

If so, in which kind of situations do you do so?
And with which kind of people?

For further reading

'The Church and Money', Frontline B20, Church of Scotland, Department of Education.
NB The materials on money produced by the Stewardship Department of your denomination.

6 Taking care of yourself

Every home has situations needing pastoral care. They may not become obvious until there is a crisis, but they are there.

In chapter 5 we looked at some of the situations you may have to face as a district elder. In our busy society many people do not receive the time and attention—the care—they need. An elder who finds the time, and who knows how to care for people can make such a valuable contribution in terms of the questions and feelings people have. *We can, however, be hampered by our feeling of inadequacy and weighed down by our sense of responsibility.*

It is important to recognise, and to accept, our ultimate helplessness in the face of another person's pain. The acceptance of this is crucial. It can set us free from the need in us to prescribe remedies. It can help us to concentrate on offering what is ultimately far more helpful—a caring presence.

Paul refers to this positive helplessness when he says—'When I am weak, then I am strong' (see 2 Corinthians 12:7–10). Unfortunately many of us interpret our feeling of weakness as inadequacy and certainly not strength and so our helplessness becomes a negative, rather than a positive, thing. We therefore face conversations moving into deep waters with anxiety and foreboding. Even before we enter any deep waters, simply in contemplating what we are called on to do as elders, we feel inadequate.

Feeling of inadequacy

Feelings of personal inadequacy have various roots:

1 We may suffer from the results of society's conditioning which has persuaded us to choose to be more aware of our weaknesses than of our strengths. Often it seems to us that other people are more capable than we are; that we should leave it to them. Many of us,

There is much more to you than meets even your own eye!

generally speaking, do not have a very high opinion of ourselves. Contrary to popular opinion, pride is often not our problem. It can be the lack of it—the lack of an adequate sense of our own worth.

- Remember that when you feel inadequate, it does not mean that you *are* inadequate. You may have accepted someone else's opinion for that a long time ago, and lived it out as though it were accurate. For many of us, growing up in the world of the 'big people', with its many parental put-downs (even in the best of homes), was not easy. There may be many things about which we could usefully think again—including our own sense of self-worth and potential. That is also something to remember about others as we care for them.
- It is also good to remember that you, and they, are children of God, 'made in God's image and likeness' (see Genesis 1). There is therefore much more to you than meets even your own eye!

2 We may set ourselves up to feel inadequate by having false expectations of ourselves. If we see our task as carers to be the giving of authoritative answers and solutions, the removal of pain and suffering, then we have set ourselves an impossible expectation. Failing as we must, added to our feelings of inadequacy, can crush us.

Remember that giving answers and solutions is not your main task. Your task is to *be with* another person in their difficulty (and in their joy) and to communicate that caring presence through your listening and responding.
Recognise that you do have caring skills and that these can be developed.

3 The feeling of inadequacy can also arise from a feeling of unworthiness, based on the false belief that, to serve God, we need to be worthy of that calling.

- Your calling does not depend upon your worthiness, but upon God's grace—God's acceptance, understanding, forgiveness—God's call. You have not chosen yourself for this work.
- You have been chosen through the selection and ordination process carried out by people who have recognised in you God-given talents and potential.
Remember, too, that so many of the leaders of God's people in the Bible were clearly flawed people; people inadequate in

many ways, but people through whom God could achieve much. Through their weakness God's strength was able to work. What he did with their co-operation, he can do with your co-operation.

Responsibility

The eldership is often described as a 'high calling'—and rightly so, because we are given high responsibility—responsibility from 'on high', for the spiritual welfare of a congregation and its locality. It is entirely appropriate that we feel keenly this responsibility. We dare not take our eldership lightly. We know that much damage has been done by those who have seen eldership as a mark of recognition for services rendered or as a status symbol. But when the sense of responsibility connects with a sense of personal inadequacy eldership can become a crushing burden.

The following maxim may be helpful:

I am responsible for doing the best I can;
You are responsible for how you respond.

It is a safeguard against apathy and perfectionism on our part.

God and your high calling deserve the best you can give. Though never a condition of his love, God no doubt looks to all of us for our best at any given point in our development. He does not however expect the impossible! He has promised to be your companion, to be with you as you try to be with others. He also goes before you and is present in every situation into which you enter. The doing of your best is something which he shares with you. He will help you to discover within yourself a 'power for good' that you 'did not even know you possessed' (Loukes quotation p 17).

The maxim is also a safeguard against the apathy of others. You can be doing your best in your district work but seeing little return for your efforts. 'Yes, I'll be at Communion on Sunday', 'Yes, I'll become more active in the life of the congregation.' Promises are made to you but are not honoured. It is common to feel that somehow it is our fault. 'Where have I failed?' you ask yourself.

Remember, you are responsible for your caring; others are responsible for what they think and do in response to your caring.

Choosing feelings

We all choose to feel what we feel.

It is useful to note that *we choose how we feel*. People can *invite* us to feel good or bad by what they do and say, or don't do and don't say, but it is we who choose how we are to feel and respond. We have the power to choose how we are to respond to discouragement.

Take, for example, this book. You may tell us that you think it is a poor piece of work and that you got little from it. We will have a choice to make. We may choose to feel very discouraged and never to write again. Or, we may accept the criticism and act positively on it. We could also question your judgement. After all, the fact that you may have got little from this book may say as much about you as it does about us. Your comment will *invite* us to feel something but the *choice* we make of what we feel and do will be our responsibility.

It is your responsibility in your caring to do the best you can, developing your caring skills, giving helpful *invitations*. How people respond to you is their responsibility. As an elder you have enough to do to carry your own responsibility without also carrying that of others.

It is good to keep in mind that there are many things for which you are not responsible, among them:

- Other people's expectations of you.
- Understanding everyone and everything.
- Liking everyone.
- Agreeing with everyone.
- The decisions and the mistakes of other people.
- Making people believe or 'come to church'.

In the end, responsibility is the ability to respond. Our responsibility as elders is to exercise the ability to respond to the call of God and to care for the needs of others as best we can. We leave to others what is their responsibility and to God what is his responsibility.

Praying for yourself

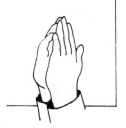

The importance of praying *for* those whom you are about to visit has been emphasised (chapter 2), as has the importance of being ready to pray *with* those whom you are visiting (chapter 4). Prayer is also an important part of taking care of yourself.

Prayer is not just asking for things, even if what you are asking for are good things for other people. Prayer is about being open to God who meets you where you are and at whatever stage you are. Being open to God is finding a way to help you be aware of God's presence with you, and to respond to that in whatever way is appropriate to you. On p 83 you will find some suggestions which may help you do this.

There are different levels of prayer similar to John Powell's 'Levels of Commmunication' (chapter 2)

- *Level 1*: Many people pray cliché prayers—the childhood prayers like 'Now I lay me down to sleep . . .', or the Lord's Prayer in parrot fashion, or the rattling off of some ritualised sentences.
- *Level 2*: Some people pray the prayers of other people—using various books of prayers.
- *Level 3*: Some people will compose their own prayers but these prayers will conform to certain theological ideas and will have a particular pattern and language.
- *Level 4*: A deeper level of prayer is engaged in when the expression of feelings is most important—feelings of praise, thanksgiving, joy; feelings of anger, sadness, fear. Many of the Psalms are good examples of this level of prayer.
- *Level 5*: The deepest level of prayer is one in which words are seen as less necessary. It is prayer in which we rest in the presence of God, but first, we need to find a way of being at peace because God says in the Authorised Version's translation of Psalm 46, verse 10: 'Be still and know that I am God.'

Prayer is a great resource. It is an opening of a door for God to give you what you need.

Jesus taught us:

> Ask and you will receive
> Seek and you will find
> Knock and the door will be opened to you
>
> Matthew 7:7

God wants us to ask for what we need. That includes what you, as an elder need as you go about your pastoral care.

Prayer is an opening of a door for God to give you what you need.

For thinking through

It is helpful to choose a story of Jesus in which he relates to another person. Read and re-read the story without wondering too much about its implications and meaning. When you have got the story in your mind, close the Bible, sit comfortably in your chair, and shut your eyes. Take one or two slow breaths—breathing in peace and quiet and breathing out tension and tiredness. Every time you breathe out feel your body relaxing more and more.

When you feel relaxed and at peace imagine yourself as present in the story of Jesus which you have been reading.

Just be a member of the crowd and watch the story unfolding. Look at Jesus, see how he looks, what he does, how he relates to people. Hear what he says. Perhaps you can imagine yourself going up to him and saying whatever you want. Listen for his reply. Give yourself as much time as you need and do not censor or interpret what goes on.

You may find this quite difficult to do, but a little perseverence with different stories may lead you to discover a new and powerful way of praying.

Some helpful passages which may be used in this way:

Jesus calls Levi	Mark 2:13-17
Jesus heals many people	Matthew 8:14-17
Jesus heals a paralysed man	Matthew 9:1-7
Jairus' daughter and the woman who touched Jesus' cloak	Mark 5:21-43
Jesus calms a storm	Luke 8:22-25
Jesus visits Martha and Mary	Luke 10:38-42
Jesus and Zacchaeus	Luke 19:1-10
The Walk to Emmaus	Luke 24:13-35

It may be that you decide to be on the shore of the Sea of Galilee or on a hillside with Jesus. Spend some time imagining the surroundings, the sounds, the smells—then imagine being with Jesus. Walk or sit with him, talk with him, or be silent. Don't direct your thinking. Let your imagination create a scene where you are led into the presence of the Jesus who is alive today.

Afterwards, when you have left the scene, open your eyes and look around your surroundings, spend a few minutes reflecting on the experience.

Working on your faith

A difficulty expressed by many elders is having to talk about what they believe. Some are afraid they may be asked questions about the Christian faith or the Bible which they cannot answer.

You can only speak for yourself. As a Christian it is more important that you can demonstrate the acceptance, love and forgiveness of the Gospel than be able to quote from Genesis to Revelation and to explain the intricacies of theology. However, most elders find it helpful to be able to put into words what they believe and their reasons for being a Christian. As with other Christians there will be times when our faith is shaken and we doubt some belief we may have held for a long time.

It is necessary therefore that you continue your own Christian learning. There are many courses offered to elders as well as courses on Christian belief for anyone interested. You can read some of the many books on Christian belief and practice. You could sit in on a New Communicants group or join a Bible study group. It is also important to find out what your denomination has said about controversial issues such as divorce, abortion, nuclear war, unemployment. If you disagree with what the Church has said on these issues you should be able to say what the Church's position is and why your beliefs are different.

Above all, read your Bible regularly with the help of a good commentary. This will aid your understanding of its background, language and meaning.

Knowing your church

It is important that you are well informed about your local congregation:

- What is happening in its lifestyle.
- The opportunities open for involvement and the points where help is currently much needed.
- Who is in charge of what.
- What the minister has been preaching about.
- News about individual members (excluding gossip).
- The past story of the congregation (particularly helpful when visiting elderly members who have belonged to the congregation for many years).

And about the wider Church:

- Presbytery and Assembly news and issues.
- Other denominations.
- Media coverage of Church interests.

Managing your time

There are few experiences more frustrating than not being able to control your own timetable. Think of how you feel when you have planned to do four visits in one evening, but you are late getting home from work. You rush out and all through the first visit your mind has not caught up with your body. You feel that it has not yet arrived at the house! Then when you are about to leave, the woman whom you are visiting begins to tell you about a painful experience she has had that day, and you know you will not get any more visiting done that evening.

It is important to be realistic about the number of visits you can do in an evening—and to allow for emergencies. Have some kind of timetable in your head, having taken into consideration the people you are going to visit and what their needs and expectations are likely to be. Be ready to adapt and change.

It is helpful to spread your visiting out over the year. Decide how often you are going to visit each family in the normal course of events, *ie* excluding visiting because of illness or other special reasons. If, for instance, Communion is celebrated quarterly, spread your visits over the intervening three-month period. It may be helpful for you to set aside one evening per week or fortnight for visiting. If you decide on your timetable, and stick to it, you will guard against rushing your visits and so setting up yourself and those whom you visit, to feel frustrated. But remember to be ready for the unexpected.

You may also find it helpful to programme variety into your visiting—so that on any one evening all your visits are not being made to young families, or to old folks or to people who are not interested in the church. After what you expect to be a difficult or frustrating visit you may wish to visit someone who will warmly welcome you and in whose home you can relax.

You may find some members more welcoming and enjoyable to be with than others. Again for your own well-being, and that of the people you are visiting, it can be useful to plan a balanced number of visits and to make the last one, if possible, to someone with whom you feel comfortable and valued. By saying this we in no way imply that you should spend more time with, and give more attention to, those with whom you feel more at ease.

Working along with others

In Romans 12 Paul describes the relationship we have, or should have with our fellow-Christians. We are 'members one of another'. We can take care of ourselves by realising that we do not work alone. All God's people share a common ministry (chapter 1). This is true of the worldwide Church and should be very much so of the local congregation—the basic unit of the Church. This being so, then elders are not meant to work alone. We are not just individual elders but elders together modelling God's care. The Session is your support group—its elders 'joined to each other' in mutual support, encouragement and learning.

For further reading

Free To Be Myself, Ann Warren, Hodder and Stoughton, 1986.
Handbook to the Bible, edited by David and Pat Alexander, Lion, 1973.
Introducing the Bible, William Barclay, Christian Education Council, 1977.
User's Guide to the Bible, Chris Wright, Lion, 1984.
The Daily Study Bible Series, William Barclay, The Saint Andrew Press.
'Teach Yourself Material: Pack One', Frontline Target Pack, Church of Scotland Department of Education, 1988.

7 Caring for each other as elders

We turn now to something we consider crucially important—how, as elders, we care for each other. Ask yourself how you care for each other in your Session?

Pause for a moment and list the things your Session actually does to foster care for each other and to demonstrate that care.

You may have found that a difficult thing to do. Not many Sessions, at least in our experience, think very much about this. This is unfortunate for many reasons, including the fact that there is likely to be a close relationship between how the elders care for each other and the care they together give to their congregation and neighbourhood.

Consider the following axioms:

- *Christian ministry is a shared ministry*: We showed in chapter 1 how all who belong to God's Church have a ministry to care for each other (fellowship) and together to care for those 'outside the faith' (mission) (p 20). We stressed the importance of the witness of the local congregation in this.
- *Leadership is about achieving goals:* The role of the Session as the leadership team of the local congregation is of crucial importance in the Presbyterian tradition (p 22).
- *Achieving goals has a lot to do with how we care for each other*: Effective Session leadership has much to do with how the elders work together and how they care for each other. The development of what we call a *caring Session* is therefore of great importance.

It is recommended that this chapter of *Caring for God's People* is read in conjunction with *Leading God's People*, chapters 2, 4 and 5.

Selection procedure

Caring for each other as elders begins with the *selection* process, the manner in which we call people to the eldership.

To ask someone to become an elder is a serious matter:

- For the person.
- For the Session and congregation.
- For the neighbourhood.
- For the people the elder visits.

Selection must be done prayerfully and carefully. We must appoint people who are mature and maturing Christians, people of whatever age or sex who have leadership skills. Those to whom a district will be entrusted must have pastoral skills. A caring Session will certainly not appoint people on the 'any elder is better than no elder' principle, just to get visiting of the districts done.

Selection must be done unselfishly. The good of the person being considered is a key factor. A person may clearly have the necessary qualities but there may be this or that in their life (*eg* family commitments, starting a new job *etc*) which would make an approach at this point in time difficult for the person, perhaps even unfair. A caring Session will consider this.

Preparation programme

A caring Session will give those it does invite all the time and help it can to assist them in coming to a meaningful decision. It will provide the best *preparation programme* it can—explaining the job and with no fudging of the challenge and the commitment being asked for. It is clear to us that there are many elders who feel they were cheated at this point—'It wasn't really explained to me what was expected'. There can be a fear of fully explaining the commitment in case the invitation is declined. To proceed along such lines is dishonest and uncaring.

An honest preparation programme should be offered and offered in an open-ended way which allows the person at the end of it to decline the invitation with the same openness if that is the decision. On p 89 you will find an illustration of what one Session developed in these two aspects of care.

Bellfield model

Selection procedure

The Session had always used the method of electing elders by nomination and decision of the Session itself. Any system is open to error but we saw no reason to change this procedure. Together, however, we evolved the following decision process.

At the Session meeting following the one at which it had been decided to add to our numbers, names were suggested for prayerful consideration but on the clear understanding that no discussion would take place at this stage with any of the people concerned. There is no need to embarrass someone by a rejection.

It was agreed that the election would take place at the next meeting of Session.

On the evening of the election Session reminded itself of three things:

1 The confidential nature of what was to take place and that any breach of confidence would require to be explained to the Session. It is vitally important that each elder feels free to speak as he/she feels.
2 The importance of what we were about to do, not least

for the people we might ask to consider taking the vows of eldership which are akin to marriage vows.

3 There being in our judgement no precise number that required to be reached, the people who would be nominated were in no way in competition with each other.

Nominations were then called for with a brief comment to justify the nomination. A list was formed of those who received a seconder.

Attention was then given to the first person on the list.

The nominator and seconder were invited to speak. Full and frank discussion followed. When Session felt ready to undertake the first vote each elder was able to vote:

For the nomination,
Against the nomination,
Don't know that the time is right,
Don't know the person.

The 'Don't know the time is right' category permits support but real pastoral concern for the person's present family circumstances, work situation or whatever else might place too heavy a burden on the person at this particular time.

The 'Don't know the person' allows escape from a 'For' vote simply because it appears unkind to oppose a nomination.

The vote of the Session was charted for all to see. Then came the second vote. Each elder voted 'Elect' or 'Not elect' on the basis of judgement of the strength of Session opinion.

Before the voting had begun we had decided that if, for example, there were 22 of us present 19 'Elect' votes would be required for a person to be approached. And so we moved slowly down the list.

These evenings were not short but for all of us they were moving and fascinating experiences and had a bearing on the subsequent integration of new elders into the team.

This procedure rarely led to many approaches being made to people at any one time but it meant that people were approached when the whole Session really believed them to have the potential to become committed and effective elders.

Procedure in outline
Session meeting: decision to elect
Session meeting: possible candidates listed for consideration.
NB no approaches to be made

Session meeting: **election**
three reminders: importance, confidentiality, no fixed number and decision re second vote.
Nominators — seconders —>list (brief word)
(fuller word—supporting statement—discussion)

First vote: Yes; No; Not at this time; Don't know the person

Second vote: Elect; Not elect
Final decision

Individual interviews (with minister) (1):
Unspecified time for consideration

Individual interviews (2):
Further time if required

Individual interviews (3):
decision as to whether or not to embark on open-ended preparation course

Preparation course (five meetings)

Individual interviews (4):
Further time if required

Final interview (if required)

Session meeting: Report. Decision *re*: Ordination date. Time span: at least six months.

Ref. *Leading God's People*, p 58.

Contract

When elders are ordained they are asked to declare their belief in the 'fundamental doctrines of the Christian faith' and to make various promises. The following example is taken from the Church of Scotland's Book of Common Order (1979):

> Do you believe the fundamental doctrines of the Christian faith: do you promise to seek the unity and peace of this Church: to uphold the doctrine, worship, government and discipline thereof: and to take your due part in the administration of its affairs?
>
> Then shall each answer: I do.
>
> After the question has been answered to the satisfaction of the Session the formula shall be signed by the elders-elect.

It can be helpful, and caring, for a Session to provide a written *contract* which spells out in more detail what it expects in fulfilment of what are often very general vows, *and* what it in return will give to the elder. A contract is, like a covenant, a two-way thing. An illustration of such a contract is given below. The provision of such a contract is an expression of real care.

For thinking through

The Elder's Contract

I affirm the following vows I took when I first publicly proclaimed my faith:

. . . .
. . . .
. . . .

I am prepared to take the following vow(s) of ordination as laid down by my denomination:

. . . .
. . . .
. . . .
. . . .

SESSION MATTERS

Contract—or just a chat?

What kind of preparation programme were you given for your decision 'yes' or 'no' to the call to the eldership? What kind of contract, written or implied, did you enter upon?

The situation is changing but many elders admit to little more than what they call 'a chat with the minister'. Many of them I think feel cheated by this.

This may also explain in part the kind of comment—'I've been an elder for years. I don't need any training'. This may cloak fear. It may simply reveal ignorance. It is certainly a great discouragement to many of the new elders.

Elders who came in on an unwritten contract and with little preparation, with the implication that there is little more to the role of an elder than some basic duties and routine church maintenance—despite the considerable oratory in which the little may have been couched—need our special attention.

As more and more elders and sessions are developing their work, wanting to play in a higher league, requiring more of their team, it has become apparent to me that we have to take care of those who came in on a lightweight contract. It is not fair, let alone loving and productive, to point an accusing, parental finger at them. They did not contract to play in a higher league. They therefore require and deserve the opportunity, however it is done, to re-contract—to contract *in* to the new expectations or to contract *out* and with dignity.

At a very basic training programme in one Presbytery an elder at the end of the course said: 'This training is good. Why wasn't I given this before becoming an elder'? I agreed that that was a good question, but, having established that he had been an elder for a number of years, during which time his Session had appointed other elders, I asked: 'What kind of preparation did you give them?'

Now that you are an elder and part of the vitally important selection process, what do you and your fellow-elders offer by way of preparation and clear contract? If it is little or nothing—'a chat with the minister'—the responsibility, or irresponsibility, is a shared thing.

In so doing I affirm my desire, with the help of God and my fellow-Christians, to live as a Christian in all the aspects of my life, outwith as well as within the Church.

As an expression of my love for, and loyalty to, Jesus Christ and his Church I accept the call to be an Elder and as such to join the Session of

. . . .

I promise to play my full part in the work of the Session:

> at its (monthly) meetings;
> on its Sunday welcoming rota *x* times a year;
> in its Communion Sunday duties as required;
> in its work of leadership where my talents appear best suited;
> at its in-service training programmes held *y* times a year.

I accept the following specific area(s) of responsibility:

. . . . *(eg* the pastoral care of a district)

. . . . *(eg* education working party).

I promise to be loyal and caring towards my fellow-elders and minister.

I recognise the life-long intention of this commitment.

I accept that specific areas of responsibility given to me may change from time to time according to the needs of the Session.

Signed . . . .

Date . . . .

- What do you feel about a contract like this and its possible value?
- What do you feel about asking for it to be signed?
- Compare the above with the Church of Scotland practice on p 90.

SESSION MATTERS

Counting the cost

The work of an elder should be at least as much as that of a B B officer or Sunday school teacher, that is, over and above our Sunday duties, at least an evening a week devoted to our work as leaders of a congregation. In an average month this could mean participation in the session meeting and that of the congregational board. A valuable evening could be spent in a district (or combined districts) house group. One or perhaps two evenings could be given over to district work, thus unshackling pastoral care from pre-Communion visits only.

Do I hear you say that you already give far more than an evening a week as it is? It may be that you are also a B B officer, Christian Action group leader or whatever. Perhaps your husband or wife often says: 'Why don't you just take your bed down to the church halls?'

Is it right that you are doing so much? Is it a good management (stewardship) of your time?

Perhaps elders who are given heavy, time-consuming responsibilities in the congregation, or who are playing a major role as Christians in life beyond the congregation, should be offered a small district or no district at all, for their own good and the good of a district they may not be able to care for pastorally. Perhaps as Sessions, and as individuals, we have decisions about priorities to face up to.

Unfair burden

Come with me to the AGM of a congregation's men's club—a fun club, carpet bowls and the like. A man is being pushed into becoming its treasurer. He doesn't want the job but no one else is willing, despite the fact that few of them give much time to the working life of the congregation.

The man is a good elder. He has his Session and board meetings to attend. He has his district to care for. He is a Bible class leader and does much else to help his congregation. He has his everyday work and, not least of all, his family to look after and be with. Here he is being almost bullied into taking on yet another commitment. The whole thing is very unfair. If the club cannot produce a treasurer for its lightweight activity, without placing another burden on a fine elder, I question its value in the life of the congregation.

We may have to make value judgements and say no to some involvements—even if it means that this or that in the life of the congregation has to collapse— so that time and energy can be given to what matters more.

A mistake we can, consciously or unconsciously, make is that of holding all the jobs in the hands of the few. An analysis of this can be quite sobering. Try it out for yourself. Sometimes the few want it so. They need it so. You can watch various congregations slowly dying in the hands of such leaders who do not even begin to grasp that Christian leadership is about encouraging and enabling the ministry of others.

Of course it isn't always easy to obtain the help of others, especially after years of the control of the few, and so we opt for the line of least resistance. Someone resigns from a not too onerous task. An elder has just retired. He is asked to take on the task. He already has at least one other demanding job in the life of the congregation on top of his eldership, but it is easier to ask him than to go out into the congregation and find someone not already overly committed. If the elder agrees, as so often we do, the few have again added to their burden, at cost to family, to health, to the more important aspects of our calling as elders, and at the cost of many in our congregations who do not feel needed and wanted at the heart of the working life of the congregation.

SYMBOLS OF LOVE

Caring selection procedure
Good preparation programme
Clear contract
Position playing and job sharing
In-service training
Structures for mutual support

Position-playing and job sharing

You will notice that the contract on p 90f mentions areas of responsibility. A caring Session will develop a participatory management style—giving people space to exercise their talents and creativity, matching tasks to skills and enthusiasms. At the same time it will take great care not to give even the apparently 'willing horses' too many responsibilities. If necessary, some jobs will be put on 'hold' until enough people can be found to share the load.

In-service training

The importance of *in-service training* has long been recognised in many fields. It cannot be less important in the work of caring for God's people. Many elders, rightly or wrongly, feel inadequate in visiting the bereaved, answering questions about the Bible, expressing faith in difficult and often complex life situations. We all need help in developing our understanding, our skills, our confidence. A caring Session will therefore encourage its elders to take part in courses held at national training centres and in courses held in the Presbyteries and Provinces.

At these courses horizons can be widened as elders from different situations share their experience. A caring Session will *also* provide its own courses and opportunities at which its elders can get close to each other as they explore some aspect of their work. Individual and collective skills can be developed. We say *also* because training in the different situations mentioned are complementary opportunities, not alternatives.

A caring Session will have an 'education and training budget' for this skills development and confidence building. Money will be earmarked for this.

Mutual support

It is unfair, let alone thoroughly unChristian, to give someone a responsibility (*eg* care for a district) and to leave the person to get on with it unaided and unsupported. To do so is to demonstrate a lack of care for the person and indeed for the task given. We all have our weaknesses, as well as our strengths. We all have our failures (real or imagined) to cope with, as well as our strengths to be affirmed. We all need *support* which helps to accentuate the positives and cut down the negatives.

Carers need to be cared for. The role of the minister in the care of the leaders of a congregation is vital, as is their care for the minister. A caring Session will have *mutual support* high on its agenda, as capital 'B' business.

An elder and his/her family ought to have an elder other than the one who is a member of the family. Every elder's family can benefit from the caring ministry of another elder who is less emotionally involved. The skills we talked about in chapter 3 can be hard to exercise in our own homes! Our emotions can so easily get in the way. A helpful structure to try to ensure real care for the carers and their families can be the appointing of what has been called 'elders' elders'. In a Session of, say, 26 elders two experienced and trusted elders could each be given as their district 13 elders and their families. Such a structure would be *an expression of love*—a structure for mutual support, a tangible expression of the care the Session wants to give to each of its elders.

The provision of learning and training opportunities and the provision of mutual support are closely related.

By 'learning' we mean developing awareness and understanding of, for example:

- The faith and its implications for our day-to-day living.
- The Church and the purpose of the local congregation.
- The role of the Session, *etc*.

Self-awareness and awareness of other people are important elements in any learning process.

By 'training' we mean developing skills like:

- Listening.
- Recognising and stopping the roles and games we and other people play to the destruction of good relationships.
- Caring effectively for the bereaved and those suffering life's many loss situations.
- Encouraging others to talk about faith, pray together etc.

As people learn and train together, if the opportunities are well conducted, they get closer to each other, becoming more aware of each other's strengths and weaknesses and the reasons for them.

SESSION MATTERS

'Knowing each other'

I invite you to think about the members of the Session you belong to. Assuming that you are sitting comfortably and safely as you are reading your *Life and Work*, take a moment or two to think about your fellow elders. Close your eyes and visualise each of them.

Did you miss any of them out?

Are you uncertain about some of their names?

If you belong to a small Session, and especially if you have been on Session for some considerable time, your answer to these questions may well be 'of course not!' If you belong to a large Session your answer may be 'Yes' to both the questions.

But consider, even if you know all of their names, how well do you know them as people? Do you know their life situations, their joys and enthusiasms, their difficulties and sorrows, why they tend to behave in this or that way? Without this kind of knowing our work of leading the congregation together will be impaired.

Do you know what your fellow elders feel about their eldership? Are they enjoying it? Do any of them feel over-burdened? Are some being imposed upon by being allowed to carry more than their fair share of the work? Are any taking on more church work than they should for their own good, their family's good, the Church's good?

Do some of them feel out of their depth in their district work—feeling inadequate in bereavement situations, in situations where they know there is a need to put their faith into words, or whatever?

Without this kind of knowing one another how can we care for each other, be the Church to each other?

On a district visit something happened to one elder. It so shattered him that he resigned. Whether or not the resignation could have been prevented at the time I do not know. What I do know is that it was many years later before some of his former fellow-elders found out what had led to the resignation. Had their Session been more aware of each other, more caring for each other, the experience might have been shared at the time and the pain level for the person concerned reduced.

Do you feel known, understood and valued by your fellow-elders? Do they feel known, understood, loved by you and by each other?

The result of this, in our experience, is the deepening of the ties that bind our hearts in Christian love.

The process is greatly helped if we work not only at *'head' level* but also at the *'heart' level*. (p 32, levels 4 and 5). There are, of course, times for working at the 'head' level—the intellectual level of information, opinions and judgements. There are times for working at the 'heart' level—of sharing experience and feelings.

It is worth pointing out that, while we may *respect* a person for the quality of their intellectual ability and knowledge, we *love* a person whom we know at the deeper *'heart'* level and by whom we feel known, understood, accepted—loved. Our decision-making can be done far more effectively when it follows sharing at the 'heart' level.

On p 97 you will find some examples of things you can do with your fellow-elders at the 'heart' level. Despite the initial embarrassment which can be felt by people unfamiliar with this kind of sharing, the experience is almost invariably well received. On training courses with elders from different Sessions we have received many comments like 'It was enriching to share good experiences', 'It was a relief to share', 'Why can't we do this kind of thing in our Session?' Why indeed! From elders who belong to the same Session we get similar positive comments. More than once we have heard—'I have learned more about a fellow-elder in the past few minutes than I have in the past five years.' We are not surprised.

This kind of sharing clearly produces warmth and affection, understanding and support. There is celebration in the sharing of good things and relief in the sharing of 'failures' when elders actively listen to one another. The will to work hard and well together is encouraged.

It may be that you are fortunate to have a particular friend on the Session with whom you can share your feelings. There may be other elders who do not. A caring Session will structure opportunities for all of its members to experience this mutual support.

We are not advocating forcing someone to 'bare his soul' or 'wear her heart on her sleeve'. Sharing can begin where people feel comfortable and are free to opt out at any point. Love does not force itself on anyone. Jesus did however make it clear that he wanted his followers to love one another. For love to grow we have to open the boxes of our life to one another—to know and be known. This we can do gradually as trust and confidence grows. There would be a lot less stress on ministers, elders, and members of the congregation if there were more opportunity for people, in appropriate ways, to share their experience and feelings.

A Session which works together at the 'heart' level will practise the listening skills we talked about in chapter 3. It will experience the deepening of its togetherness. It will be encouraged to try to foster this in its congregation and the experience will greatly benefit its pastoral work.

The cartoon illustrates a group of people who have not yet learned to come out from behind their masks and roles. They do not know each other. They only know the images they have of each other. They will have difficulty in making decisions and even more difficulty in implementing them. Absenteeism from meetings will be high. Loyalty to one another will be low and mutual support virtually non-existent. One shudders to think how they would select and prepare other people to join the group.

For thinking through

Examples of working at the heart level

The   Δ   = the Church
         ⌾   = you

1   Share in groups of 4–6 which picture most closely represents the way you feel about the Church and why this is so.

The same thing can be done by thinking of the triangles as being your eldership, or your district.

2   Invite everyone to recall a 'good' visit each has made as a district elder.

By a 'good' visit is meant whatever each feels to have been enjoyable, meaningful or whatever.

Pair up, calling one person A and the other person B. A shares the visit with B who, for two or three minutes, *listens* and, without taking over the conversation, provides good attention.

Reverse the roles.

This can be followed by a sharing in the same way of visits felt to have been 'bad'.

Before this is done a *contract* can be taken out by each saying to the other 'Whatever I hear in the next few minutes I will share with no one without your permission.'

Debrief the experience, paying attention to the feelings and the value of the sharing.

E

We find it most encouraging that more and more Sessions are developing the range and depth of their work. We draw your attention, however, to a concern that we have that goes along with this development. We refer to the difficulty, even distress, that some elders who were brought in on a lightweight contract may feel as the life of the Session deepens.

Sometimes we are asked, 'How does an elder resign?' Is this, we wonder, a cry from the heart, demanding more than the simple answer: 'Ask your Session to accept your resignation and to remove your name from the ranks of the eldership in your denomination'? Underneath the question may lie many feelings that need to be cared for: feelings of *guilt* about giving up; *fear* of what others might say or do; *tiredness* born of having been given too much to do in the life of the congregation; *inadequacy*, real or imagined.

These negative feelings can reveal themselves in absenteeism or in obstructive behaviour, objecting perhaps 'on principle' to things about which it would be difficult to oppose on Christian principles.

A caring Session will recognise the symptoms (though they will be less likely to appear in a caring Session) and will try to get to the cause—for the well-being of the person as well as the good of the Session.

The problem may not be so acute in traditions which have made active eldership a terminable appointment. Where this is not the case voices are sometimes raised calling for a change to terminable appointments. We would resist this because we think of the vows of ordination as being akin to marriage vows. We would not wish to see marriage vows which said 'I will love and cherish you . . . for the next five years . . . with an option of another five years if both parties agree'! Marriage and the commitment to the crucial role of the eldership require a more long-term commitment, as indeed does the commitment to what is called 'the full time ministry'.

Though divorce is now rife—clearly a bad thing for society—it is perhaps good that the stigma attached to divorce is lessening. It has been responsible for keeping many a 'marriage' going at a cost far out-weighing the good of those concerned. It is sad when people who once took the vows of marriage to each other feel they have to seek divorce—and especially so when it is made a bitter, acrimonious and

For thinking through

What kind of preparation programme did you receive when you were first asked to become an elder?

Was it adequate?

What would you have liked to have had included in it?

What practical help were you given when you began to care for a district?

Was it enough?

What might it have usefully included?

What are you providing for those whom you invite and ordain to the eldership?

Is it enough?

Is there anything that you could usefully add?

What help and support are you providing for each other as members of your Session?

● ● ●

If on a visit to the home of one of your members you were asked how you can believe in the love of God in the face of the world suffering we see on television almost every evening, what would you say?

If a young person asked you to recommend a good, but not too difficult, book to help him or her to understand more about the Bible, which book would you suggest?

If someone asked you what you felt Christian faith said about euthanasia, how would you respond?

What would you say to someone who asked your advice about taking a job in the nuclear arms industry?

If a non-member described himself as a Christian, not because he knew much about Christ, but because he believed himself to be a good person, what, knowing him to be a 'good' person, would you say?

If you were asked 'What does Jesus mean to you?' what would you say in reply?

What other questions cause us difficulty?

How are we, or could we be, helping each other to be able to respond to such questions as Christian leaders?

If someone says that such questions do not arise for us as elders, then you might consider why that is so. If it is the case, there is something wrong somewhere!

graceless experience. In some circumstances, however, despite the seriousness of the step, divorce may be the better way.

We look at the eldership in the same light. If, for whatever reason, meaningful eldership is beyond repair, resignation may be the better way. If this is the case let it be done gracefully and with the support and understanding of the partners. Perhaps breakdowns in both areas would be less if there had been better *preparation* for, and *support* throughout, the *contract*.

A caring Session, following some of the guidelines we have suggested and getting to know its members at the 'heart' level is more likely to recognise the symptoms and do what it can to help those who feel under stress. It will love its members enough to let those who feel they can no longer fulfil their vows out, and with dignity.

Further expressions of love

Assessment

Some elders may seek to resign, not because they are inadequate but because family or work commitments have altered and increased, preventing them from giving the time they need—and still want, to give. A caring Session will provide regular opportunities for *assessment*—times when its members can take stock, collectively and individually, about the Session and their part within it. Through this, and other means, a caring Session will find ways of adjusting its workloads.

Re-contracting

As standards go up and expectations increase (which does not necessarily mean an increased time commitment) a caring Session will provide opportunities for *re-contracting*—either contracting in to the new agreed expectations or contracting out by those who feel they can no longer continue on Session.

Sabbatical leave

In traditions where elders are appointed for life some may seek to resign, not because they feel inadequate and want to resign, but simply because they are tired and need a break. Such people could be offered release from their duties for some given period of time. Sabbatical leave could be built into our care for each other.

We would not recommend total release because we feel it is important for the elder to stay abreast of the Session's thinking and to retain the sense of belonging. Such a person could continue to attend the main Session meetings, but be free of all other duties for the given period.

Sabbatical leave could, for some, be offered as a time free from normal duties, but a time in which to do some learning and experiencing. With the help of the minister and one or two other elders, the person could be helped to work out some (not too demanding!) study programme.

For example: a distance learning course, or a self-programmed course of Bible study, or reading material about the faith, some aspect of the ministry of the Church, *etc*, participation in training courses provided for elders at national training centres or at the Presbytery or Province level. For a district elder time to develop pastoral skills could be very helpful.

An elder on sabbatical leave might be encouraged to study something of particular interest to him or her, or, if willing, to engage in a piece of research which the session could find helpful.

We realise that this would take some organisation but it is not beyond the capabilities of most Sessions. Some of the difficulties which will come readily to mind have to be faced in many other areas of life where the principle has long been operated. Sabbatical leave could enable an elder to return to normal duty with new ideas and renewed enthusiasm to the benefit of all concerned.

Confidentiality and loyalty

Someone once said: 'It was a mistake to discuss my alcohol problem with my elder. It came back to me that she had criticised my behaviour with other elders.' That was a most damning comment. The elder may have betrayed a confidence. His fellow-elders certainly let all concerned down. Matters like confidentiality and loyalty to each other cannot be over-stressed. Nor can they be imposed. They are the product of a Session which has become a caring Session.

SESSION MATTERS

'I just told my elder . . .'

You are in a member's home. Eventually the conversation gets round, if not to the sharing of faith, at least to church matters.

Someone starts to get critical. On Sundays the prayers are too long. The sermon is boring. Perhaps the minister or a fellow-elder comes in for criticism about some mistake he or she is said to have made in a particular situation. Faced with this, what do you say or do?

Test this out for yourself. When you are being negatively and hurtfully critical about someone or something, you may sound thoroughly rational and objective, but inside, beneath it all, you are feeling bad about something. When you are at peace, when you are feeling happy, you sometimes cause hurts by mistake, but you do not do so intentionally.

If this is true, then, when faced with hostile criticism, we need to try to get beneath the surface to the feelings. It may be that the critic had a bad experience during the war and felt God or the chaplain had not met their need. This bad feeling has been nursed and fed throughout all the intervening years and on this pastoral visit it has surfaced for those with eyes to see and ears to hear.

It may be that the person had a particularly good relationship with a previous minister or elder and is going through the process of bereavement and has not yet been able to adapt to the new situation.

Perhaps the person sees himself as a 'failure' and has longed, without success, to achieve some status in the life of the congregation.

We need to help the person to get in touch with the real feelings which underlie the bitter criticism—and to confront him or her, gently, in time, with the real issues.

Constructive criticism, which will be conveyed in an entirely different spirit, we will welcome. The late Norman Swan, once wrote: 'We who sit in the pews are not to be regarded as amiable peasants, uninterested in Christian plans and with little to offer.' We can receive constructive criticism—without disloyalty to our fellow church leaders or to the critic himself.

It would be hard, however, to over-emphasise the importance of loyalty to one's fellow-elders, past as well as present. This is not to say that we have to defend each other as pure and faultless human beings, which clearly we are not.

But it is to say that we take care not to fuel the winter of people's discontent. Even our interested silence can be used as fuel. 'I just told my elder what I thought. He didn't disagree.'

The role of the minister

Before we conclude this chapter—a word about the role of the minister.

The role of the minister in any Session is crucial. We understand it principally to be about *leadership*—the kind of leadership which *enables* the others on the Session team to realise their God-given potential, discovering their gifts of leadership and finding their niche within the work of the Session. This, as we have said, is a shared responsibility, but the minister's role as Moderator of Session is central.

The minister should not assume, nor be expected to assume, the role of pastorally caring for all the members of the congregation, though of course, the minister has a full part to play in this. Collectively the Session should be able to provide more and better care than could ever be provided, at least in a fair-sized congregation and locality, by one person. It is important for elders who have a district to have a close working relationship with the minister. The care of the leaders of the congregation will be a priority concern for the minister.

Caring for the minister

A minister can be in a very vulnerable position, as can the members of his or her family. For some it is a lonely and isolated position. This can be very much so for an unmarried minister. A caring Session will do all it can to ensure that this is not the case. It will, itself, be a support group. Within the limitations of our human frailty the elders should give their minister 100 per cent loyalty (not the same thing as dutiful agreement) and vice versa. If we cannot look to each other for real support where, in God's name, are we to look?

A caring Session might establish, as part of its pastoral strategy, a particular structure in this regard—a small support group of people who will, in the strictest confidence, share the difficulties (and hopefully the joys) of the minister and those who live in the manse. This would be another expression of love.

A Session which works on the kind of things we have suggested in this chapter will become more and more of a caring Session which its members will rejoice to belong to. It will provide better pastoral care for its congregation and at the same time encourage the members of the congregation to become part of a more caring congregation.

SESSION MATTERS

'Burn-Out'

As you will know, there is a lot of concern in the Church at the moment about what is termed 'ministerial burn-out'. It prompts one to ask—How does your Session care pastorally for the person or family who live in the manse?

I remember my early days as a parish minister when, with Shakespeare's Shylock, I felt 'prick me I bleed'—a feeling you may sometimes also share as a district elder.

I wonder what the 'elder burn-out' rate is.

We can feel the object of the prayer 'Bless Thy minister and elders, *our servants*'.

What a difference it makes when as members of Session we get to know each other at the level of our feelings and shared experience, the soil in which love for one another can flourish.

Depth of caring

One of my most treasured memories is of conducting a particularly difficult funeral. I was trying to be God's servant to a family who had lost their son in a tragic accident. By the time this happened love and under-standing had become something very real for us as elders. By then my fellow-elders knew what it cost me to try to minister in this kind of a situation.

I will never forget the family standing in the front row, holding each other up and singing 'On Christ the solid rock I stand, all other ground is sinking sand'— the hymn we had chosen together. Nor will I ever forget the presence, not just of the family's elder, but of 50 per cent or more of the Session present to be a strength to me, to minister to me.

After the service Andrew returned to his factory. Fifteen minutes after his shift ended, around 10.15 pm, if I remember correctly, there was a knock at the manse door. The manse elder had called just to check up on how I was feeling—the incar-nation of the prayer 'Bless our minister, *Thy servant*'.

With more of this kind of depth of caring for one another there would be far less need to talk of 'burn-out' regarding ministers or elders—or indeed of members of our congregations.

For thinking through

Expressions of Love

- Caring selection procedure
- Good preparation programme
- Clear contract
- Position playing and job sharing
- In-service training
- Structures for mutual support
- Assessment
- Re-contracting
- Sabbatical Leave
- Confidentiality and loyalty

In answer to the question, 'How do you care for each other in your Session?', how many of the above would you have listed?

On a scale of 1–5, rate your Session's performance in regard to each of these aspects of care for each other.

What recommendations would you make to improve your score?

In preparation for chapter 8

How might your level of care for each other as elders be affecting your pastoral work—individually and collectively?

How as a Session do you organise your pastoral work?

8 Developing a pastoral strategy

When a Session is asked to explain its present pastoral strategy, that is, how it organises its care of the congregation, the elders can be a bit perplexed. If they find an explanation difficult to give, it is not because they do not have some kind of a strategy, but because little thought has probably been given to it. What has been done in the past has simply been continued uncritically.

Common practice appears to be as follows:

- *The congregation is divided into districts or groups*. This is often done on a geographical basis. Often the lapsed members and the unchurched receive little attention.
- *Elders are appointed to get these districts covered*. The central factor in the number of elders on Session is likely to be the number required to cover the districts. Check this out in your Session. One or two elders, for example the Session Clerk, may be 'relieved' of pastoral duties. 'Relieved' is a telling word! It points to the fact that the one or two, and it is likely only to be one or two despite the fact that the primary role of the Session is leadership, were originally brought on to Session to look after a district.

   Despite this control factor little clear thinking may be given to the nature of pastoral care. This can be particularly true when pastoral care is closely linked with the delivering of communion cards. If little thinking is done about the nature of pastoral care, it is likely that little attention is being paid to the pastoral skills of the people being appointed. A person may be a regular worshipper and may have served on some congregational committee but these things do not mean that the person will be an effective district elder.
- *Elders are left to get on with their district*. A district elder may receive little or no support from the Session. In many Sessions there is scant provision of confidence-building training

opportunities designed to develop pastoral skills. Rarely is an attempt made to check up on whether or not the district elder is providing effective care.

Common practice is based on a very limited and inflexible system which ignores many important factors, including some of the things we talked about in chapter 7.

A good pastoral strategy has, as we have stressed, to be based upon careful elder selection and preparation procedures. It will have built into it ongoing in-service training and mutual support structures to care for the carers. A caring Session will want to consider some of the following factors in the development of its pastoral strategy.

Time availability and size of district

Real pastoral care takes *time*. It is ridiculous to expect most elders to have the time to care for 30 homes. Whistle-stop tours might be possible, but not ongoing care. A good strategy will take account of the available time of each elder and therefore also the *size of district*—the number of homes given to each elder. Included in this will be consideration of geographical issues and what is expected in terms of concern for lapsed members and non-members in the district.

Flexibility

Putting together questions of time and size of district, a caring Session will also recognise that, not only will elders have different time availability, but that this can vary for any elder from time to time. An element of *flexibility* may have to be built into the strategy. It could help with a problem that most of us have to face, namely that there are some homes in which we have tried to do the things talked about in chapter 3, but the chemistry just did not work. The possibility of exchanging calls could be very helpful to all concerned.

Specialisation

This leads us on to another factor. We all differ in our abilities. Some of us are better at caring for elderly people than are others. Others of us may be more effective with young married couples or with single people who often feel isolated in our family-orientated congregations. Some of us may be gifted in the winning back of the

F

lapsed or in encouraging the non-believer to begin to consider our faith. It would be a pity to place elders who have this talent in a district largely consisting of elderly people who have enjoyed a life-long faith.

Some elders might be asked to specialise in what is sometimes called 'pastoral evangelism'; modelling God's care in the homes of the unchurched at the points of contact often provided by times of crises.

If we are to think about *specialisation* it may influence not only the size of the districts, but how we construct them in the first place. The geographical factor may not be the only criterion that is used.

As we begin to think about these factors we begin to see how they impinge upon each other. Different kinds of districts may require different amounts of time. A district of elderly, and perhaps lonely people of whatever age, may call for many more hours to be spent in it, and daylight hours at that.

Elder deployment

We will want a variety of people and skills on Session. We might want a Christian town councillor to provide expertise about local needs and how we might help. We might want a Christian youth and community worker to help shape our youth programme. With their work in the community these people may not be able to undertake also the care of a district. The same may be true for the B B captain or the leader of the Sunday school.

A caring Session might consider pastoral work as itself a specialisation—calling for expertise and training—and deploy certain elders to this work. When elders are given too many jobs one of the casualties is likely to be district care.

Deployment of other people

If some of the above factors are taken seriously, and we do not make pastoral work the single control factor regarding the appointing of elders, then it is likely that we will have to include in our pastoral care strategy the use of members of the congregation.

If we follow the understanding of shared ministry outlined in chapter 1, then we will in fact want to deploy, under the supervision of the Session, the talents of people who may not have the leadership skills required of elders, but who are not lacking in caring skills.

It may not be possible to implement fully all of the factors we have

For thinking through

Pastoral strategy

Are there any obvious weaknesses in the way you organise and carry out your pastoral work?

Consider the following factors relevant to a pastoral strategy:

- Caring selection procedure
- Good preparation programme
- Clear contract
- Expertise
- In-service training
- Mutual support
- Time availability
- Size of district
- Flexibility
- Specialisation
- Elder deployment
- Deployment of other people

How might your Session build in, or develop, any of these factors?

Identify any areas in which you would welcome some training.

Decide how you will get that training.

outlined. A caring Session will, however, do what it can to develop, bit by bit, a better strategy than the common practice outlined on p 104f and that it will do so by considering these factors. The fact that some Sessions are doing so indicates that what is being suggested is neither impractical nor impossible.

The following district teams structure permits many of the factors to be put into practice.

District teams

Instead of the one elder/one district structure larger districts can be constructed, each served by a team of three or four elders. Each team member can be given particular responsibility for certain homes within the area, but along with other team members can share concern for the whole area. The more geographically compact the membership and the area served by the congregation, the easier this is to establish.

Entirely new areas can be delineated or three or four existing adjacent districts can be combined, taking into account geographical and social criteria, the number of homes of members and the total number of homes in the area. Time availability, different skills and the ability to work together will be considered in the forming of each team of elders.

Each team can have one of its number appointed for a stated period of time to act as the *team convener*. The choice of convener may be made on the basis of leadership skills and relationship skills or, assuming at least competence in these areas, on the basis of more time availability. A convener could be released from some other piece of work to provide time to fulfil this important role.

The convener's role

This can include the following:

- Pastoral care for his/her own part of the enlarged area.
- Assisting and encouraging the team (particularly important regarding new elders).
- Ensuring continuous pastoral coverage of the area.
- Chairing team meetings.

Maintaining up-to-date information regarding the area (changes of address, offers of help *etc*).

Maintaining good two-way communication between the team and the minister or church office.

The agenda of a team meeting

This will include the following:

- Sharing information, concern and prayer for the people of the area.
- Mutual support in difficult pastoral work and personal problems.
- Discipline (though the final word remains with the Session).
- Area projects (subject always to Session approval).
- Deployment of non-elders, encouraging the assistance of members of the congregation in pastoral work, magazine delivery, flower distribution, acting as street look-outs to aid contact with new people in the area, helping with door-to-door visitations and area projects *etc*.

The teams can meet during one or two normal Session meetings or, on occasion, team meetings can replace the normal Session meeting so as not to demand extra time. They can, of course, also meet at other convenient times if they so wish.

This team structure will, as we know from experience, incorporate and encourage a good pastoral strategy.

- An elder whose life has become complicated and who cannot for the moment cope with all (or any) of his or her visits can have these visits temporarily covered by the other members of the team.
- An elder who now requires, for whatever reason, a smaller district can, if the team cannot make the necessary adjustments, transfer into a team which can release an elder to take over a larger district.
- An elder who is unable to get on well with family X may exchange the call with a team member who is making little headway with family Y.
- The team structure also permits a degree of flexibility in the deployment of elders according to special skills—working with the lapsed etc.
- The team structure can even help the matter of sabbatical leave.

For thinking through

District teams

The Bellfield model

This illustrates one Session's attempt to provide a less limited and more flexible strategy than its previous one elder/one district practice.

Twenty-five elders' districts were reduced in number to eight enlarged districts, covering the whole neighbourhood the congregation was called upon to serve.

Each enlarged area was looked after by a team of 2, 3 or 4 elders, each of whom had his or her own calls, but who together cared for the enlarged area.

Each team had one elder who acted as its convener. Convenerships changed quite regularly.

The teams could meet as and when they liked but all or part of two Session meetings each year were given over to team meetings to save further time commitments.

The Convener's role and the agenda for a team meeting are outlined on p 107f.

List the possible benefits of a district teams' structure:

THE PARISH OF BELLFIELD, KILMARNOCK

Council housing estate
Population c 7000
† = St Ninian's
Sc = Local primary school
Sh = Local shops
G = Gardens and playing fields
RC = Roman Catholic Church
S = Salvation Army
M = Mormon

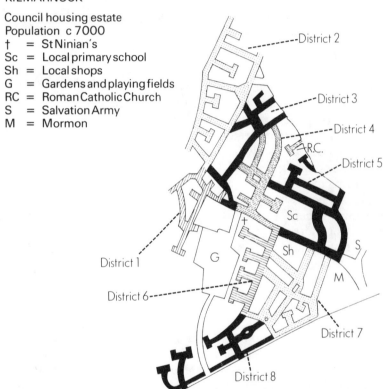

- To the individual elder, including a newly appointed elder.
- To the members of the congregation.
- To the work of the Session as a whole.

List the difficulties you feel about developing such a structure.

What would it require of a Session to be able to implement such a structure?

9 A caring congregation

Various people stress different things on which they feel the Church is needing to concentrate more. For example:

- Getting more people into the pews.
- Encouraging greater commitment from members.
- Developing more effective communication.
- Changing out-worn traditions.
- Conducting livelier worship.
- Finding more 'ministers'.
- Raising more money.
- Having better buildings.
- Showing more social concern.
- Getting more politically involved.
- Putting greater emphasis on adult education, on evangelism and mission, on Church unity.
- Developing our prayer life.

These are all vitally important issues, but there is a need to be tackled—one which underlies all these other needs—and that is to develop our congregations as *caring fellowships*. Care, or love, is the mark of the Church rather than what we believe and profess. Love is the real witness to our faith because it embodies what Christian faith is about. The Word of God becomes flesh in our loving.

Individual caring elders together form a caring Session which has the responsibility of *enabling* the congregation it leads to be a caring congregation.

This concluding chapter provides a few pointers to some of the essentials in the lifestyle of a caring congregation which is trying to be God's people in its locality.

Fellowship

In a caring congregation its members will be offered the opportunity to care and to be cared for. Its members will be helped to feel that they belong, are valued, and have a real part to play in the shared ministry of the congregation. If these needs are not met people may not feel greatly committed to the Church and are likely to view it as a *place* to which to go, frequently or infrequently, rather than as a *family* or *community* to which they belong.

The support of the fellowship of a caring congregation is necessary for each individual Christian. This surely was part of the reason Jesus brought the Christian community into being, promising his living presence in the midst of those who gathered *together* in his name (Matthew 18:20).

It is in the laboratory conditions of the Church in its local congregations that we can learn and grow, mature and become the people God would have us be; the people we have it within us to be—with the help of God and each other.

We draw your attention to chapters 12 and 13 of 1 Corinthians.

In 1 Corinthians, chapter 12, Paul speaks about gifts of the Spirit. He says:

The Spirit's presence is shown in some way in each person for the good of all (v 7).

He goes on to use the analogy of the human body to talk about the nature of the Church, especially in regard to the local congregation. He points out that the strength of the body lies in the different parts, each with a different function, working together. He points out the need for acceptance of those who differ from us, and of those who are weaker or less attractive. He talks about the inter-relatedness of the members.

There is no division in the body, but all its different parts have the same concern for one another. If one part of the body suffers, all the other parts suffer with it; if one part is praised, all the other parts share its happiness (v 25ff)

He says:

All of you are Christ's body, and each one is a part of it (v 27).

This is, of course, the same teaching as in Ephesians, chapter 4 (p 20). As members of the Church we are all part of a *shared ministry*.

In 1 Corinthians, chapter 12, Paul lists some of the gifts given to different members of the Church and advises us to set our hearts on the more important gifts. He then says:

Best of all, however, is the following way (v 31).

He goes on in the following beautiful chapter to talk about love, without which—no matter our other strengths as individuals and as congregations—we are nothing.

The Church's unity thus depends, not on uniformity of gifts or functions, nor on agreement or even understanding, but upon the quality of our love. We are effective as Christian individuals, Sessions and congregations when we are struggling above all else to be loving. This is because love is the gospel we proclaim and all else in the Church must be secondary to that. We are called together to love one another as Christians and together to love those who are 'outside'—to love *all God's people*.

'Fellowship' is an over-used and under-valued word in the Church vocabulary. It is often offered at a very superficial level in the life of a congregation. Opportunities to experience it at deeper levels need to be offered. Fellowship—sharing at the 'heart' level as well as at the 'head' level—needs to develop and grow until we discover how it is that we can begin to relate to each other openly, honestly and caringly—learning to drop our masks, barriers and inhibitions. John Powell's 'levels of communication' (pp 30f) need to be applied to the fellowship life of the congregation. As openly and lovingly we communicate with people, on the level where they are while being ready to move levels, we begin to model the kingdom of God.

SESSION MATTERS

Bringing the generations together

I get very nostalgic at Christmas when, in lots of different ways in our congregations, we celebrate the birth of Jesus. My mind returns to one of the happiest occasions in the calendar of my former congregation.

In most of our congregations, as well as the special Christmas services, we hold Christmas parties for the children. But are 'children only' parties enough? What about the elderly, especially those who have no family around them? The festive times for the lonely can be particularly difficult. But are 'elderly only' parties enough? Should we not be thinking more about our congregations as family units and be planning events which bring the generations together?

Out of this thinking was born our Christmas singalong. All ages came—young children, lots of teenagers, the elderly and all stages in between. It was really much more than a singalong. Our evening began in the sanctuary where we worshipped God happily together. Then all who wished to take part went through to the decorated hall for a candle-lit supper—a modest but nonetheless a full three-course affair, the food having been gathered in collectively. It was a beautiful sight to see the family of our congregation so obviously enjoying each other's company in this setting.

After supper we entertained ourselves. It was simple home-spun fun with lots of people involved in leading the entertainment. It ended with the singing of some of the songs of Christmas—hymns ancient and modern. When the benediction was pronounced it was done so within a community which had expressed itself as a family.

From this there were developed other family occasions. The very special Easter Sunday Communion in the spring attended by our children; the summer outing after morning service to the beach, requiring two buses and a fleet of cars to transport us to the shore; the church family lunch in the autumn.

Francis Schaeffer has written 'Our churches must be real communities . . . They have largely been preaching points and activity generators. Community has had little place . . . . Every Christian Church should be a community which the world may look at as a pilot plant.'

There's a lot to think about in these words. You might care, in your Session meeting this month as part of your celebration of the birth of Jesus into a family to think about how you demonstrate the family togetherness of your congregations.

Mission

At the end of Matthew's gospel we have Jesus' clear instruction to go into all the world to encourage discipleship:

- Sharing our answers to life's religious questions.
- Sharing our faith in God and his 'abundant wealth' to supply all our needs.
- Sharing our faith in the new beginning made possible in Jesus to all the inhabitants of the 'garden'.

Jesus said:

If you have love for one another, then everyone will know that you are my disciples (John 13.35).

Jesus would have us lay great stress upon the developing of caring congregations—and not just for our well-being!

Christianity is not only about God's care for the individual person, but also about his care for the world and the shared life of all its inhabitants. The Church therefore is not only about loving individual people, but also about demonstrating *a new way of living in community*. The Church is meant to model bound together—by God's love society, reaching out to God's world. This is particularly true of the basic unit of the Church—the local congregation.

We will win the world when we realise that fellowship, not evangelism, must be our primary emphasis. When we demonstrate the Big Miracle of Love, it won't be necessary for us to go out—they will come in.

Jess Moody

Jess Moody may have been overstating the case, but the point he is making is highly relevant. What is the point of all our activity, our orthodoxy, our full churches and organisations if there is no caring fellowship?

Jesus said:

I have chosen you to be with me. I will also send you out (Mark 3:4)

The Church is called to be with Jesus—to be his community and then to be sent out from that base to care for and share with others. Fellowship leads to mission and, as Jess Moody implies, caring fellowship is itself an aspect of mission. A caring congregation is the presence of the 'body of Christ' in the midst of its locality.

Christian mission is only 'Christian' when those who go out do so from the base of a sharing fellowship and whose style and methods of mission are caring and accepting. Christian mission is not only based on valuing God, but also on valuing those to whom we bring the 'Good News'. It is not only about listening to God, but also about listening to those to whom we go.

The vitally important link between fellowship and mission is also brought out in the following quotation.

> To think of 'Christianising the world' exclusively in terms of getting certain principles accepted, or certain values accepted, or even in terms of getting individuals to have a relationship with Christ, would be to miss one of the basic realities of human nature that—human beings do not function independently; they change in groups. The target has to be to form Christian communities . . . . It is necessary to form communities within society to make Christian life possible.
>
> Stephen B Clark

Mission needs to be seen not only in terms of evanglistic meetings or door-to-door visiting, but in terms of the development of what we have called 'caring congregations'.

Service

A caring congregation knows in Jesus' answer to the question 'Who is my neighbour?' that its neighbour is whoever is in need, in the neighbourhood and on the opposite side of God's world. (Luke 10:25-37). It will find much work to do. There will be no difficulty in distinguishing it from St Marmaduke's (p 121).

It will be a *listening* congregation, using its collective eyes and ears to recognise where need exists. As Jesus did, it will identify itself with human need—with those who cannot find satisfying answers to life's questions; with those who live under dark clouds of bad feelings; with those deprived and under-privileged.

It will *check out* what it has heard and seen and try to *respond* in ways which are constructive, which help people to discover their worth and God-given potential.

'Day after day they met as a group in the Temple, and they had their meals together in their homes, eating with glad and humble hearts praising God and enjoying the goodwill of all the people. And every day the Lord added to their group those who were being saved.'
(Acts 2:46f)

A Christian should keep faith—but not to himself!

RICH WORLD

POOR WORLD

The Great Divide
as seen by Tear Fund

'I tell you this: anything you did not do for one of these, however, humble, you did not do for me.'
(Matthew 25:45)

It will distinguish between symptoms and causes in an individual, a family or the wider society. It will share God's concern when a major employer threatens closure or a strike threatens the future of the area; when children lack school books and social services are not being adequately provided; when the Third World needs food and a fair share of the world's wealth.

The issues may be complex and Christians may differ greatly as to the causes and what they understand to be a genuine Christian response. In a caring congregation, led by a caring Session, we shall be able to differ but still be able to demonstrate God's care for his world and all its peoples.

A caring congregation will express its faith (be evangelical) with sensitivity. It will know that there are times and situations in which the Gospel can only be expressed meaningfully in actions. It will learn when and how to share its faith also in words.

Worship

The Sunday gathering of a Christian community to worship God together and the taking part in the Sacraments which show God's love for all his people, will reflect the things we have been thinking about.

Christian worship in a caring congregation will be:

- *Warm*: modelling its togetherness in Christ, which is deeper than differences (biblical, doctrinal, organisational) that may be held.
- *Participatory*: modelling the variety of gifts God has given to His people for their shared ministry.
- *Intelligible*: expressed in language and symbols and music which are meaningful, easily understandable, in tune with their day, modelling a faith—for yesterday, today and tomorrow.
- *Welcoming*: modelling God's care for *all* his people ('Session Matters,' p 116)
- *Colourful and lively*: modelling God's *'inexhaustible'* vitality'.

There will be times:

of joyful praise and thanksgiving
of wonder and awe and mystery
of silence to reflect and to listen
of challenge and of comfort
of expressing concerns
of confession and re-dedication
of learning and sharing

SESSION MATTERS

Not uncaring—
just careless

My wife and I were given a wedding anniversary present by our daughter—two tickets for an Everley Brothers reunion concert. That dates us, as it did the rest of the audience! As we entered the auditorium, having had our tickets cut in two by a disinterested person, the usherette looked at us and let us pass by to search for our seats unaided. It was a cold welcome to the theatre.

We enjoyed the show. No doubt the theatre owners and staff and Don and Phil Everley, were glad we were there to receive our ticket money, but we came and went with no attention paid to us. No one knew we were there—and no one really cared about us.

Entering a sanctuary to join in the worship of God should be a very different experience. With all that our faith teaches us about God's love, Christian togetherness, concern for the stranger, one would expect a real warmth of welcome. Even if the minister bids all welcome from the pulpit, it is important that members of the congregation somehow express their joy in sharing this time of worship together.

As elders we should be encouraging this.

For many years I had the pulpit to pew view. The pew to pulpit view can be a very different one. Like ministers, office-bearers have their place, their status, their Sunday duties. We are 'at home' but we can be blind to those who don't have our involvement. The stranger or fringe-member—perhaps someone seeking to find the way 'home'—can be overlooked. We don't mean to be uncaring but we can be careless.

When on door-duty I trust we are never like that usherette, but we can get engrossed in conversation with our fellow office-bearers, enjoying each other's company, transacting church business, and the stranger can pass by with barely a glance or with a brief "Good Morning".

After a warm welcome at the door it would be good to have an elder in the body of the sanctuary to reinforce the welcome and to offer help, if it seems appropriate, to find a pew and perhaps someone with whom to share the fellowship hour of worship.

We would not wish to force ourselves on anyone but people should not be able to come and go with no real attention paid to them, feeling that no one knew that they were there and no one really cared.

I STILL SAY-
YOU'LL NEVER
GET ME UP
IN ONE
OF THOSE!

Small groups

One of the difficulties for the average congregation is that it is, in many respects, too big. We need to meet in smaller groups if we are to get to know and care for one another. The Sunday worship (which we think of as the large group gathering) does not, as a rule, provide the best opportunity for caring for one another—though it can happen to some degree before or after the service. If caring is basic to the life of a congregation it must dictate the kind of structures we have and what goes on within them.

By the small group gathering we mean the opportunity to meet in groups small enough to permit a getting to know each other by name, in a way that we cannot in the large group. These small group opportunities can be held in the homes of members, where there can be generated a real caring for, and sharing with, each other; where they can not only talk *about* the Church but *be* the Church to each other.

> House groups are not just 'yet another meeting for busy people'. They are gatherings where busy people and others are recharged with fresh energy to go on loving.
>
> Jean C Morrison

As fellowship grows so openness to learning together will also grow. As someone once said: 'You don't need to feel stupid because you know the people around you love you. You gain confidence.'

In house groups a congregation can bridge the generation gaps which it sadly often reinforces in its organisations. Through these groups the lapsed can be helped to find a point of re-entry.

As satellites out from the main church building they can be of value in reaching out to those 'outside'. Some people who would not dream of coming to a recognised church building will be prepared to come to the home of a Christian friend to share in a Christian group. The house group can also express practical Christian service to the homes in the streets around where it meets.

Recent developments in mission and younger church areas—especially the group movements in India and elsewhere—have shown us that we must recover this group approach and free our traditional mission work from Western individualism. The same plea is made also by those who stand on the evangelistic frontier of the industrial society in the West. The 'house church' is an answer to this plea.

Hans Ruedi Weber

There is great value in offering the experience of belonging to a small group. It lay at the heart of the life of the early Church. It has been at the heart of most Church revivals. It is natural for Christians to gather in small groups.

It can be offered in a wide variety of ways and with different emphases—worship, fellowship, learning, outreach. There are a number of issues to consider carefully—the purpose of the groups, programming in tune with the chosen emphasis, the leadership and the support of the leaders, the structuring of the groups and their relationship to the life of the whole congregation.

'Where two or three . . . .'

Some of the unscripted comments of people who take part in the house churches in the congregations of St Ninian's Bellfield Kilmarnock and St Mungo's Cumbernauld.

'We get the Gospel explained to us in the Sanctuary. If we are really going to try and live it out then the house group is the place where we can start. Then we can move further into the community and try and live the Gospel with the strength we get from the groups.'

'The main part is encouraging participation and getting to know each other, to share problems . . . . In time we get back round to the subject matter but I think the emphasis is on relationships.'

'I found that by joining the house group I got to know the people better and now when I go into St Ninian's Church I know the people there and there is always someone to speak to and it makes you feel wanted.'

'No disrespect to our own minister, or any minister, but he could stand up there and preach for two hours, but by going to a house group you feel that you are at the same level . . . . You get

a better feeling and more understanding when you are all together. You are not just a Sunday worshipper. It carries on all week after.'

'What I find is the trust that we have in the people in the group because very often you speak innermost thoughts that you have never spoken to anyone else, but you do in your group, and they listen and they help you.'

'When my wife was in hospital the house group, prayed for Margaret and I think through that I got the strength to carry on and the feeling I got out of that was that I wasn't alone.'

'When my husband died I was absolutely shattered of course but the support that I got from the members of the house group was just tremendous. It gave me a great feeling, them sharing with me . . . it helped me tremendously to have that support. When you are a member of the group you feel that there is a great sharing no matter what happens to anyone within the group.'

'How seldom is a congregation given the opportunity to share its faith with each other . . . Minister to congregation relationship is one thing . . . but the house group is a tremendous opportunity for small numbers to share with each other and what a difference it makes to the district elder. What a tremendous opportunity he has to get to know the folks in the district as they share together . . . . House groups, too, have been good for the leadership. They have brought them out . . . increased confidence in themselves.'

'One important thing we have found . . . is the placing of the house group . . . We have used them to bring in people who may be on the fringe of church membership . . . . They have come into contact with the Church in a real way again . . . Very often you will find that the husband who maybe doesn't go to church regularly stays around for the meeting . . . sometimes older teenagers stay around.

For further reading

Growth Groups, Howard J Clinebell, Abingdon, 1972.

Building Small Groups in the Christian Community, John Mallison, Scripture Union, 1978.

Creative Ideas for Small Groups in the Christian Community, John Mallison, Scripture Union, 1978.

Grow to Love, Jean C Grigor, The Saint Andrew Press, 1980.

Face to Face, Gerard Egan, Brookes/Cole, 1973.

'For Developing Church House Groups', Frontline Target Pack, Church of Scotland Department of Education, 1987.

'For Developing A Congregation's Education Committee,' Frontline Target Pack, Church of Scotland Department of Education, 1987.

Making Adult Disciples, Anton Baumohl, Scripture Union, 1984.

'Discussion Material for Elders:' Pack One, Frontline Target Pack, Church of Scotland Department of Education, 1987.

'Developing the Missionary Parish', Work Pack, Church of Scotland Department of Ministry and Mission, 1988.

'Parish Review', Work Pack, Church of Scotland Department of Ministry and Mission, 1988.

Mission Guides Leaflets, Church of Scotland Department of Ministry and Mission.

> 'Caring for the Lapsed'
> 'Caring for New Communicants'
> 'Reaching the Men'
> 'Preparing for Parish Visitation'
> 'Sharing our Faith'
> 'Rural Evangelism'
> 'Evangelism through Pastoral Care'
> 'Evangelism in Small Groups'

'Do We Care Enough to Share? Strategy for Evangelism, Irish Presbyterian Church Board of Evangelism and Christian Training.

Restoring The Link pamphlets, Irish Presbyterian Church Board of Evangelism and Christian Training.

> 'Active Church Membership'
> 'Church Attendance'
> 'Christian Commitment'

A powerful structure for the small group opportunity is to locate it in the enlarged Elders' districts (pp 107ff). The elders' team can share the leadership to the benefit of the Session's life and teamwork and to that of the congregation. Such a structure offers every member a place in a house group in the same way as they have a place in the large group. The return can far exceed the effort required.

As with the large group opportunity, the small group opportunity is central to the life of a caring congregation.

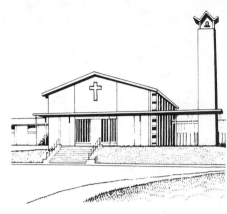

A local church and its buildings symbolise God's care for *all* his people.

The Session

The collective role of the Session, including the district work of its elders, is crucial to the development of a caring congregation.

What we have called a 'caring Session' will provide a *model* for its congregation in this regard. It will develop structures and strategies ('symbols of love') and put into operation in the life of the congregation the kinds of things it has itself first done to develop its own togetherness and skills. It will do all in its power:

- To prepare people carefully and prayerfully for active membership, with the expectations clearly stated for new members and those coming in from other congregations.
- To identify the interest and skills of its members, giving them meaningful expression in some aspect of the shared ministry.
- To take care not to over-burden a few and discount the many.
- To integrate members into the life of the congregation, providing a real sense of belonging and influence.
- To provide learning and training opportunities and the vitally important mutual support ('heart level') factor.
- To offer many opportunities to celebrate being God's people.

To belong to the leadership team of a caring congregation is to be part of something infinitely worthwhile, exciting, challenging vital. It is something to be done with enthusiam.

To belong to the leadership team of a caring congregation is to be part of something infinitely worthwhile, exciting, challenging vital. It is something to be done with enthusiasm.

What other people have said about the Church

Mark Gibbs and Ralph Morton

'St Marmaduke's is a fine fellowship—indeed a cosy club of a fellowship, moving from summer tennis to autumn barbecue, and from youth dances to old folk's film shows. And yet, though all these may be worthy and admirably run social groups we have no hesitation in saying that a fellowship which consists *only* of doing such things together is quite damnable—indeed it is already damned, or condemned, by all the New Testament has to tell us about Christian fellowship together.

'The People of God are meant to show God's love to His world, not to enjoy it quietly in a cosy group on their own. They are meant to be the Body of Christ—the *embodiment* of Christ's love and compassion towards the world . . . .

'God's Holy Spirit is given to His people, not for the running of a 'happy' fellowship of Sunday and weeknight evening activities but for the agonising work of serving—'ministering' to (it's the same word in Greek) the needs of others.'

R C Stedman

'What is terribly missing is the experience of 'body-life'—that warm fellowship of Christian with Christian which the New Testament calls *koinonia*.

'In the early church a kind of life was evident in which Christians would gather together in homes to instruct one another, study and pray together, and share the ministry of spiritual gifts. Then they would go out into the world again to let the warmth and glow of their love-filled lives over-flow into a spontaneous Christian witness that drew love-starved pagans like a candy store draws little children.'

Dr von Thadden

'We must learn to serve the *world* better. We must have the courage to come out from our comfortable domestic lives and bring our faith into the dangerous, confusing and yet exciting life in the world outside the grey walls of our church buildings.

'And we must have the courage to question much that does go on within these buildings.

'To what extent do our Sunday services, our religious jargon, our methods of Bible study, our cosy spirit of fellowship, indicate to the outsider that we are a kind of private religious club (at which he will not be very welcome)?

'And to what extent does our worship and our Church life together offer him a clear message of God's forgiveness and God's concern for his daily life in the factory, the office, or the farm?

'So often a local church seems to exist for the sake of its members, rather than for the people in the streets around. We need the courage to take our Faith outside.'

Michael Griffiths

'A body in which only one member is functioning is nearly dead and taken off to hospital. The one-man band concept of the church is a cultural hangover from the days in Britain and elsewhere when the squire and the parson were the only literate people in the parish capable of reading the Bible lessons.

'Roy Castle is credited in the Guinness Book of Records with playing forty different musical instruments in four minutes: what an illustration of the omni-competent one-man band minister.

'How few congregations there are where a lot of members are exercising functions. Often the majority of members are passing spectators and auditors of the religious professional's performance.

'The Church is not a third-class

waiting room where we twiddle our thumbs while we wait for first-class accommodation in heaven. It is a dynamic new community winsome and attractive, and with an eternal significance in the purpose of God. The Bible makes it clear that the Church is God's goal for mankind, for the new humanity in its new communities.

'The salvation which God has planned is not merely aimed at producing saved individuals. We are looking for a wonderful new community and a truly great society—God's own people. In our impatience and rebellion against the institutional Church we must not throw out the biblical baby with the institutional bathwater . . . Christians are to be brought together as living stones, and put together into a new building in which God is to be worshipped . . . . There is all the difference in the world between a great heap of bricks and these same bricks carefully fitted together and built into a beautifully designed building.'

Lesslie Newbigin

'The Church is the pilgrim people of God. It is on the move—hastening to the ends of the earth to beseech all men to be reconciled to God, hastening to the end of time to meet its Lord who will gather all men into one.'

For thinking through

'We must have the courage to question much that goes on within these buildings.' (p 121)

What does go on, under the leadership of your Session, within, and from the home-base of your congregation's buildings, in terms of:

- Fellowship?
- Mission?
- Service?
- Worship?

'The People of God . . . . are meant to be the Body of Christ—the *embodiment* of Christ's love and compassion towards the world.' (p 121)

Can you identify, in the life of your Session and congregation, ways in which Christ's love and compassion are embodied?

' "body-life"—that warm fellowship of Christian with Christian which the New Testament calls *Koinonia*.' (p 121)

Discuss the body-life of your congregation. Where is it found? Is it planned for? Is it for everyone?

Share your thoughts about the following quotation:

'We will win the world when we realise that fellowship, not evangelism, must be our primary emphasis. When we demonstrate the Big Miracle of Love it won't be necessary for us to go out—they will come in.'

Jess Moody.

'The Church is the pilgrim people of God.
It is on the move.' (p 122)

Where do you see movement in your congregation?

Do you see any connection between your Session and your congregation, *ie* between the quality of your Session's caring (as outlined in chapter 7) and your efforts to develop a caring congregation (chapter 9)?

Are there steps you could take to develop either or both?

If you have the problem of non-attenders, what does your congregation need to change in order to help people feel at home at services of worship?

On the road

Throughout this book we have emphasised that caring for God's people has to do with what we believe about God. We care in his name. We take Jesus as our model. It is from him that we learn what caring is about. It is from him that we learn about the power of caring—and also about its vulnerability.

In the caring Jesus showed we see the acceptance, the challenge and the valuing of the love we are called to offer. In him we see the Word of love made flesh and from him we hear the invitation 'Follow me'.

We are invited to walk *with* him so that we may learn to walk *with* others.

In Luke, chapter 26, we are given a clear picture of Jesus—the Companion on the road.

The walk to Emmaus

On that same day two of Jesus' followers were going to a village named Emmaus, about eleven kilometres from Jerusalem and they were talking to each other about all the things that had happened. As they talked and discussed, Jesus himself drew near and walked along with them: they saw him but somehow did not recognise him. Jesus said to them. 'What are you talking about to each other, as you walk along?'

They stood still, with sad faces. One of them named Cleopas, asked him. 'Are you the only visitor in Jerusalem who doesn't know the things that have been happening there these last few days?'

'What things?' he asked.

'The things that happened to Jesus of Nazareth' they answered. 'This man was a prophet and was considered by God and by all the people to be powerful in everything he said and did. Our chief priests and rulers handed him over to be sentenced to death and he was crucified. And we had hoped that he would be the one who was going to set Israel free! Besides all that, this is now the third day since it happened. Some of the women of our group surprised us; they went at dawn to the tomb, but could not find his body. They came back saying they had seen a vision of angels who told them that he is alive. Some of our group went to the tomb and found it exactly as the women had said, but they did not see him.'

Then Jesus said to them. 'How foolish you are, how slow you are to believe everything the prophets said! Was it not necessary for the Messiah to suffer these things and then to enter his glory?' And Jesus explained to them what was said about himself in all the Scriptures, beginning with the books of Moses and the writings of all the prophets.

As they came near the village to which they were going, Jesus acted as if he were going farther; but they held him back, saying. 'Stay with us; the day is almost over and it is getting dark.' So he went in to stay with them. He sat down to eat with them, took the bread, and said the blessing; then he broke the bread and gave it to them. Then their eyes were opened and they recognised him, but he disappeared from their sight. They said to each other. 'Wasn't it like a fire burning in us when he talked to us on the road and explained the Scriptures to us?'

They got up at once and went back to Jerusalem where they found the eleven disciples gathered together with the others and saying. 'The Lord is risen indeed! He has appeared to Simon!'

The two then explained to them what had happened on the road and how they had recognised the Lord when he broke the bread.

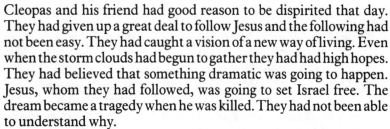

Cleopas and his friend had good reason to be dispirited that day. They had given up a great deal to follow Jesus and the following had not been easy. They had caught a vision of a new way of living. Even when the storm clouds had begun to gather they had had high hopes. They had believed that something dramatic was going to happen. Jesus, whom they had followed, was going to set Israel free. The dream became a tragedy when he was killed. They had not been able to understand why.

As they travelled home on the Sunday evening, they talked it through again, straining to find something which would make sense of it all. The only glimmer of hope was a strange story told by some of the women friends of Jesus. They said that they had been to the grave of Jesus but could see no body. They had, however, been told by angels that he was alive. But Cleopas and his friend *knew* he was dead—and yet . . .!

It was at this point that they were joined by the stranger. He was going in their direction and showed his interest in them by asking 'What are you talking about?'

His question stopped them in their tracks. It seemed incredible to them that he did not know what had been going on in the city. His question 'What things?' was an invitation to them to share their story with him.

After they had poured out their painful story, the stranger gently but strongly pointed out what they had omitted from their story. We can take it that when Jesus used the word 'foolish' he did not do so in a harsh way when dealing with two people clearly in great distress. He was helping them to bring into their loss experience the resources of their faith. Later they were able to say 'Wasn't it like a fire burning inside us when he talked to us on the road and explained the Scriptures to us?'

When they reached Emmaus, after their seven-mile walk, Jesus, making as if to go further, waited for an invitation to stay with his two companions. He did not force himself on them. When they did invite him into their home, and shared with him what they had to offer, it was then that light dawned and the truth of the resurrection became real for them. They experienced such joy and enthusiasm that, late as it was, they went back the seven miles to Jerusalem to share the Good News.

- Jesus cared for them by *being with* them—travelling the road alongside them, being where they were, entering into their sorrow and pain.

- He showed his willingness to *listen* to them. Even though he knew the answer to their question he invited them to tell him how it was for them.
- He did not rush into telling them what they should do. He *reflected back* to them what was in their heads and hearts. He helped them to bring together and examine their confused thoughts and feelings.
- He enabled them to discover the resources they already had in their experience and in their faith.
- He was *a loving presence* on the road and at their household table.

Love is at the heart of the Gospel. It is also that for which people cry in their hours of deepest need. May we as elders, caring for God's people, learn to be a loving presence with them as we journey and as we sit down with them.

- A loving presence always involves ourselves, others and God.
- A loving presence values people. It neither discounts nor rescues them.
- A loving presence listens to people, with ears and eyes—to the words spoken and unspoken.
- A loving presence responds appropriately to what it hears, allowing the other person to be responsible for their own life.
- A loving presence reaches out to the whole of the other person in warm openness and acceptance.
- A loving presence is open to finding in the other person, a loving presence.

To love is to experience God who is love. We need to experience this, and can experience it, together, within the Body of Christ in our Session and congregation. From this we learn to be the Body of Christ for *all God's People*.

Acknowledgements

The Publishers gratefully acknowledge and thank the following for their contribution to this book:

For reading the draft and comments both useful and much appreciated:

> Ronald Barclay
> Graeme Brown
> Dorothy Dalgleish
> Rowland Dalgleish
> Jenny Garrard
> David Henry
> James Hewer
> Andrew McLellan
> Jean Morrison
> Terry Oakley
> Sheilah Steven

For typing the manuscript:

> Dorothy Dalgleish
> Jean Steele

Editorial and layout by Graeme Leonard and Stewart Matthew

Cover designed by William Ross

Illustrations adapted by John McWilliam and Lesley A Taylor

Throughout the book, under the heading of *Session Matters*, various articles, written by Stewart Matthew, have been reprinted with the kind permission of the editor of *Life and Work*, the Church of Scotland's magazine, in which they first appeared.

Contacts

For information about Resources and Training opportunities United Kingdom Presbyterian Denominations contact:

Church of Scotland:
St Colm's Education Centre and College
23 Inverleith Terrace
Edinburgh EH3 5NX
Tel: 031-332 0343

Presbyterian Church in Ireland:
Director of Christian Training
Christian Training Centre
Magee House
7 Rugby Road
Belfast BT7 1IP
Tel: 0232 248424

Presbyterian Church of Wales:
Coleg Trefeca
Trefeca
Talgarth
Nr Brecon
Powys LD3 0PP
Tel: 0874 711423

United Reformed Church:
Faith and Life Department
United Reformed Church
86 Tavistock Place
London WC1H 9RT
Tel: 01-837 7661

You are invited to share your comments regarding the ideas in *Caring for God's People* with the writers who can be contacted via the Publisher.

Companion volume

What are Church Elders for? What is the job of a Session in the modern Church?

Leading God's People provides some baseline thinking about the Eldership. It applies the key ideas of teamwork and leadership to the Session. It looks at some common problems, how to manage the Session team, and how to gain ground.

Elders, and others engaged in Christian leadership, are encouraged not only to read this book as a text, but also to use it as the basis for individual activity and group discussion.

It aims to make a contribution towards realising the vast potential of the Eldership in today's Church—in enabling and directing God's people.

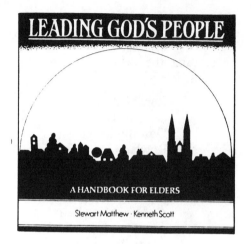

LEADING GOD'S PEOPLE

A HANDBOOK FOR ELDERS

Stewart Matthew · Kenneth Scott